There's simply no time for "Is this funny?" or "Could I do it instead in the second act?" There's a lot of discovery and freedom in this process. And of course, you have to *end* the thing.

Drama from its origins has worked hard to fire on all cylinders. Spectacle and music, costume and pageantry, and later design for special effects and all that. But underneath it all you had to have a play. Beginning, middle, end— a journey, a protagonist, a tone, a genre— and most important, as any dramatist will confirm, a successful ending. This is what makes playwrights tear their hair. This is why Shakespeare was bald.

To do all this in a ten-*minute* play? Who would be lunatic enough to enter such a competition, to create a coherent whole with something to say, well said, surprising and inevitable— while *at the same time* engaging with the past Masters of the *full*-length form... who had five ACTS at their disposal? Who would want to even try?

When you open this volume, you will find out.

Attracted by the siren song to write big, to write fast, to show their skills, to try their hands— in the colors of the more vivid and flamboyant style of the classical authors— these modern authors found that the invitation to write quick and sometimes dirty can result in something a good bit more than a sketch. When you peruse the delights within, you may find yourself savoring these miniature examples of dramatic craft with singular pleasure. These writers are both brave and strange. The gale-force wind of absolute economy drives each piece with velocity. There is no moment that is wasted, and yet there is a language tradition to be reckoned with, a faith in meanings that is distinctively pre-modern. In that combination is something perhaps ideal.

The short play and the classical play intersect in their playwrights' audacious commitment to that which makes a play a play. They essentialize the great responsibility to conclude in meaning— one that either changes theater or changes the world.

In an age of fear, a playwright must risk consequences, and in an age of anarchy and despair, a playwright has to care. Whether comic or tragic or mythic, sad or sardonic, all these writers care.

I hope you will enjoy your immersion in these works as much as I have, and find yourself, as I was, touched by these miniature worlds, ephemeral but shining in such variety and no less brave for their brevity!

Amy Freed
June 2021

INTRODUCTION

With this 5th volume of Red Bull Shorts being published (thank you, Roger & Stage Rights), we also celebrate 10 years of our Short New Play Festival! It is inspiring and invigorating to look back upon the breadth and depth of material that has been created and shared over the years. The sheer number of extraordinary writers. The wild diversity of their takes on classic material. The powerful drama and hilarious humor of the plays. The delightful variety of experimentation with form and language.

At the time of this writing, it is also impossible not to reflect upon the past year of disruption wrought by the COVID-19 pandemic and the shutdown of all our theaters. Our 10th Anniversary Short New Play Festival was of course intended to be in person, but instead we pivoted to a completely virtual/online experience. The number of plays submitted nearly doubled for the 2020 online festival from prior years. As essentially the entire world was asked to stay home, masked, and safe, playwrights who wrote for the "Private Lives" theme found themselves responding to a kind of personal solitary confinement, as well as long overdue calls for racial justice, "Zoom theatre," and more. It was (and continues to be) a remarkable time in history. These short plays provide a unique snapshot of that moment in time: Spring 2020.

Plays of heightened language are at the heart of Red Bull Theater's mission to revitalize the classics for today's audiences. When I founded the company in 2003 with the Jacobean plays of Shakespeare and his contemporaries as its cornerstone, I felt passionately that new works by living playwrights should be included in a lively conversation with the great classical writers that would form the core of Red Bull Theater's work.

To further this conversation and increase our capacity to include living playwrights at Red Bull, we began the Short New Play Festival in 2010. Each year around a given theme (revolution, greed, etc.), we commission two plays by established playwrights, and select six more through a competitive, blind, open submission process that annually receives about 300 new plays— nearly 600 in 2020. Together the eight plays are performed in an evening of work, showing off the many ways that cutting-edge playwrights are inspired by classical themes, and share a love of language and all the amazing things that it can do in the theater.

In its first ten years, our Short New Play Festival has inspired the writing of over 2,000 brand new short plays. Of those plays, we have been able to select and showcase the work of 80 playwrights. The festival has become an integral part of the annual Red Bull Theater season, becoming a source of theatrical enjoyment for a growing audience. We have also commissioned an expansion of one of our previously winning short plays into a full-length play (*The Claudias* by Lynn Rosen) and a second full-length commission in 2018: Jeffery Hatcher's new adaptation of Ben Jonson's *The Alchemist*— thrilling new developments that we aim to do more of.

RED BULL SHORTS

THE BEST OF THE **RED BULL THEATER** SHORT PLAY FESTIVAL

VOLUME V

Kate Abbruzzese
Ben Beckley
Kia Corthron
Avery Deutsch
Marcus Gardley
Terry Glaser
Leah Maddrie
Talene Monahon
Matthew Park
Eric Pfeffinger
Bridgette Dutta Portman
Theresa Rebeck
David Lerner Schwartz
Matthew Wells
Mallory Jane Weiss
Sofya Levitsky Weitz

TABLE OF CONTENTS

2019: THE EVIL PLAYS

2020: PRIVATE LIVES

A classical play is long. A ten-minute play is not. A classical play is built for the ages. It has withstood its future critics and has been anointed as enduring. But a ten-minute play is a mayfly, born to live and die in a day— and the writer knows it.

Shakespeare hoped his lines would live when he was dead, but he couldn't know for sure. Marlowe didn't live long enough to wonder out loud if his mighty lines would last, but we can bet that he hoped so. When a writer makes a play, it's in the wildly ambitious hope to see their world built or our world changed by the thought they make manifest. It's an ambitious bid for immortality, of a sort.

By contrast, a ten-minute play is an expression of— and an exercise in— ephemerality.

So, what do a ten-minute play and classical theater have to do with each other? And why is Red Bull Theatre, a premiere theater for innovative productions of the classic, inviting such an unlikely marriage of forms?

When I was asked to participate as a reader in the Red Bull's short play competition, I didn't hesitate to say yes. Everything about this theater and its mission attracts me. Red Bull Theatre is indispensable, and their work for almost 20 years has served to show that we not only can still thrill to these classic plays, but that we are hungry for the many registers of language and thought, of showmanship and poetry, that classic theater contains. Yet, although I'd contributed a short play to a previous Red Bull collection, I am not in any way an expert in the form.

In fact, in retrospect, whatever I thought about a ten-minute play was dead wrong. I assumed it was an exercise in sketch-writing, an invitation to an easy unearned ending, and didn't expect anything of complexity. What a pleasure to get an education. In the course of reading fifty plays, some good, some not so good, and some remarkable— only the remarkable are in this collection— I came to appreciate the rigor, the effectiveness, and the astonishing range of possible approaches.

Indeed, the revelation of immersing myself in these short dramatic works extended not only to my thoughts about the short play form, but to my considerations of drama as a whole. It is a form that encourages ruthlessness of attack, of economy, and of dramatic stakes. It doesn't tolerate indecisiveness. But then, to a large extent drama itself does not permit indecisiveness.

In encountering a form of a play in which every second must count, we are reawakened to the truth that in *all* plays every second must count. To write a ten-minute play is to lose all dignity to this imperative, and in the scrambling to land such a big and complicated fish in such a short time, your meanings come pouring out, your writing defenses and self-protection fall away, and essential realities come flopping on deck, thrashing and wet, perhaps, but born alive.

We've been lucky to involve some pretty incredible writers, many of whose plays are included here in this edition. In the festival's first eight years, the commissioned playwrights have been: Lee Blessing, Constance Congdon, Kia Corthron, Lisa D'Amour, Elizabeth Egloff, Amy Freed, Marcus Gardley, David Grimm, John Guare, Jeremy O. Harris, Tina Howe, David Ives, Arthur Kopit, Ellen McLaughlin, Dael Orlaendersmith, Peter Oswald, Theresa Rebeck, Regina Taylor, Anne Washburn, and Doug Wright.

Winners of the open submission competition have included: K.M. Abbruzzese, Liz Duffy Adams, Mike Anderson, Heidi Armbruster, Matt Barbot, Ben Beckley, Emily Taplin Boyd, Dave Carley, Fred Dennehy, Avery Deutsch, Terry Glaser, Dipika Guha, Arthur Holden, Will Kenton, Anchuli Felicia King, Sam Lahne, Tabia Lau, Patricia Ione Lloyd, Wendy MacLeod, Leah Maddrie, Anya Martin, Stephen Massicotte, Dakin Matthews, Elizabeth Miller, Winter Miller, Talene Monahon, Jessica Moss, Mark O'Donnell, Matthew Park, Eric Pfeffinger, Jason Gray Platt, Bridgette Dutta Portman, Amanda Quaid, Lynn Rosen, Tom Rowan, Aubrey Saverino, Natalia Savvides, David Lerner Schwartz, Jen Silverman, Tommy Smith, James Still, Matthew Wells, Mallory Jane Weiss, Samara Weiss, Sofya Levitsky Weitz, Daniel Wilson, and Tim West.

In addition to the writers, I'm grateful to the 100+ actors and directors (including such talented artists as Tina Benko, Steven Boyer, Kathleen Chalfant, Juliana Canfield, Lilli Cooper, William Jackson Harper, Louisa Jacobson, Peter Francis James, Kristine Nielsen, Linda Powell, Kate Rockwell, Jeanine Serralles, Sam Tsoutsouvas, Charlayne Woodard, May Adrales, Vivienne Benesch, Liesl Tommy, and Evan Yionoulus) who have worked with the writers to thrillingly enact and stage these plays for us at Red Bull Theater.

Ten-minute plays can be surprising and awesome. Like great short stories, they can pack a punch of drama, hilarity, tragedy, joy— all the good stuff of theater— in bite-size pieces of pleasure. I hope you are as delighted by the ones in this collection as our artists and audiences have been, and that you may find an opportunity to bring some of them to life onstage yourself.

Enjoy!

Jesse Berger
Artistic Director
Red Bull Theater
November, 2018

An Evening With The Macbeths

by

Kate Abbruzzese

KATE ABBRUZZESE

Kate Abbruzzese studied drama, psychology, and a smattering of literature and poetry at Vassar College. While there, she was selected to be a member of Vassar Improv and the Vassar Shakespeare Troupe, allowing her to speak high verse and tell silly jokes in her free time. Her senior project, playing Lady Macbeth in an all-female *Macbeth* at Vassar's acclaimed Powerhouse Theatre, earned her the Molly Thatcher Kazan Memorial Prize. After graduation, she spent four years working as an actor in regional theatre before she was accepted into NYU's Graduate Acting Program, where she received the Olympia Dukakis and Ron Van Lieu Scholarships. She has acted in 17 of Shakespeare's plays and written several of her own plays based off of Shakespeare's characters. She also moonlights as an illustrator and cartoonist. Currently, she is expanding *An Evening With the Macbeths* into a full length play.

AN EVENING WITH THE MACBETHS
appeared in the
2019 Red Bull Theater Short New Play Festival:
The Evil Plays

CAST OF CHARACTERS

LADY MACBETH. Filled to the brim with a grief which threatens to bubble over every second, but which she mostly keeps in check. Scottish accent not required.

MACBETH. A really nice guy doing his best. Tender and firm. Would make a really great dad. Scottish accent not required.

Setting: I like to think of the time period as "1950s Medieval Scotland," which means the banality of newspapers and knitting paraphernalia casually coexist with the realities of bloodshed and war. We are in the Macbeth's living room.

Running Time: Tenish minutes.

A NOTE FROM THE AUTHOR

Declan Donnellan, artistic director of Cheek By Jowl, speaks movingly of the real tragedy of Shakespeare's Scottish play: that the Macbeths are not psychopathic ambition mongers, but rather two compassionate, tender human beings who try (and fail) to kill that tenderness in pursuit of a power they aren't even sure they want.

I wrote this play because I love the Macbeths. I love the way they love each other, and I love their humanity and how it is ultimately their downfall. I wanted to get a look at that humanity: to see them as a loving couple dealing with the mystery of marriage, the tragedy of a dead child, and a life filled with separation as Macbeth goes off to battle after battle after battle.

Most of all, I love Lady Macbeth in spite of all the spirit-calling and baby-brain-dashing in her text. I've never imagined her as a power-hungry harridan nagging her husband into regicide. Rather, I think she is desperate, loving, grief-stricken, and— I have to imagine— lonely in a world where her options are to either be a mother or a witch.

4

AN EVENING WITH THE MACBETHS

Lights up on a quaint living room furnished with a rug and two comfortable armchairs. Tartan populates the space. A fire glows in the hearth.

MACBETH, kilted and cozy-socked, roosts in his armchair, reads the paper. He is a kind, gentle man. None of the brutality he exhibits on the battlefield pursues him here.

The other armchair is unoccupied. A knitting basket curls at its feet, overflowing with yarn and needles.

From offstage, a sudden sobbing. The sound of a gargantuan piece of furniture being heaved and crashing on its side.

More sobbing.

Something shatters.

MACBETH listens to all of these sounds. He does not wince, though a tender concern lingers on his face.

The sobbing and tinkling sounds of destruction diminish until they fall silent. Beat.

LADY MACBETH sweeps in, fresh faced, bearing trace of neither sturm nor drang, and goes straight to her armchair. Plucking her knitting from the basket, she drops into the chair and immediately resumes her work on a pair of baby booties. The yarn is a disconcertingly cheerful red.

She is thoughtful and concentrated, orderly and ambitious in her knitting. And totally fucking fine.

Beat.

MACBETH

Everything /ok?

LADY MACBETH

Yep!

                    MACBETH
You sure?

                LADY MACBETH
Mm-hm!

                    MACBETH
Sounded like something fell.

                LADY MACBETH
Oh, hm [that's funny].

                    MACBETH
...did something fall?

                    LADY
No.

                    MACBETH
My dearest partner in greatness?

                    Beat.

                    LADY
Yep.

                    MACBETH
Yep?

                    LADY
Yep, a few things fell.

                    MACBETH
Mmhm?

                    LADY
Your armor. Fell.

                    MACBETH
Uh-huh.

                    LADY
I sort of pushed it.

MACBETH

Okay.

LADY

And I think something else.

MACBETH

You— you think?

LADY

I'm— pretty sure there were. Somethings. Else... s.

MACBETH

Okay.
Did— anything— break?

LADY

No.
Not much.

MACBETH

All right.

LADY

Don't you wanna know what broke?

MACBETH

That's okay.

Beat. New tactic.

LADY MACBETH

Um, Mack, I wanted to ask: you're home on the twelfth?

MACBETH

Twelfth or thirteenth.

LADY

You don't know?

MACBETH

I mean, if we're lucky it'll be done by the eleventh and I'll be home early the next day. Y'know. Duncan doesn't like these things to draw on for too long.

LADY MACBETH

Okay, good.

MACBETH

Yeah, I'm hoping we're just gonna like: in, out, nave-to-chops a few guys and be done. Banquo's with me on this one so it should be pretty smooth.

LADY

Great, so the twelfth.

MACBETH

...Probably.

LADY

Okay but not *before* the twelfth?

MACBETH

No no.

LADY

Twelfth or after.

MACBETH

Mmhm.

LADY MACBETH

Okay.

Sorry if I'm— I don't mean to needle— ha— um— I'm just— I want to be sure I know when to send Ella up to give the floors a scrub? You know. It's nice, coming home to a clean castle.

MACBETH

Aw. Thanks. S'thoughtful.

> *He goes back to his paper. Another prolonged, domestic silence.*

LADY MACBETH

So, you're leaving at four tomorrow?

MACBETH

Four, four-thirty.

LADY MACBETH

Taking Harry?

MACBETH

Lightning. Harry's tired from the last campaign, needs a rest.

LADY

Goodgood. Wise. Good.

MACBETH

And I know you like Harry better so I thought I'd [leave him home for you.]

LADY

Oh, "thoughtful" yourself, that's nice.

She knits.

MACBETH

Who're those for?

LADY

Hm?

MACBETH

Those [tiny socks]— who're those for?

LADY

Oh. Um. Ella.

MACBETH

Aren't her feet— bigger?

LADY

Yes, yes they are.

MACBETH

...I'm confused.

LADY

They're not for her feet.

MACBETH

You're knitting socks for Ella but they're not for her f...?

> *She gives him a look. Recognition dawns.*

Oh. Oh!

LADY

"Oh"?

MACBETH

I— didn't know.

LADY

She's as big as a house.

MACBETH

I guess I just [didn't notice]
Hey, why don't you just give her the ones you knitted back when you were [pregnant]— for the [baby]?

> *Everything freezes. He retreats to the paper and hopes maybe she didn't hear him. She did.*

LADY

I'm surprised you didn't notice /she was—

MACBETH

I guess I wasn't paying attention.

LADY

Mm.
I guess men never do.

> *Strained silence.*

MACBETH

I wouldn't say *never*...

> *Beat.*

LADY

"Seldom"?

MACBETH

Hm?

LADY

Would you say "men *seldom* pay /attention?"

MACBETH

I don't think I'd say seldom /either.

LADY

Okay.
So what *would* you say?

MACBETH
(*lovingly diffusing a bomb*)

I'd say men. Are.
Less attuned to certain things than women are.

> *LADY regards him dispassionately. Returns to knitting. He returns to the paper.*

LADY
(*without looking up from her knitting*)

So four-thirty, then.

MACBETH

Huh?

LADY

You're leaving at four-thirty tomorrow.

MACBETH

Yes.

LADY

Not four.

MACBETH

Well... I mean, yeah, four, four-thirty.

LADY

"Well I mean" which is it gonna be.

MACBETH

I don't know.

LADY

I'd like to know.

MACBETH

Did I do something wrong?

LADY

No. I'd just like to know. Is all.

> *They lock eyes. Beat. He yields, with kindness.*

MACBETH

It'll be four-thirty.

LADY

Thank you.

> *Back to knitting. Needles click, paper rustles.*
> *MACBETH spots something on the floor.*

MACBETH

Oop!

LADY

What?

MACBETH

S'a little spider.

LADY

Eugh I'll get it.

MACBETH

Nono, it's all right, he's not hurting anyone.

LADY

I don't want to swallow him in my sleep.

> *Pause.*

MACBETH

You don't want to swallow him in your—?

LADY

You've heard that, right? The average Scot eats eight spiders a year in their sleep?

MACBETH

That can't be accurate.

LADY

It's probably more.

MACBETH

Where'd you hear that?

LADY

The Porter.

MACBETH

The Porter?! You believe something the Porter tells you?

LADY

He's well-informed!

MACBETH

He's an alcoholic!

LADY

That's—! —All right that's not untrue.

MACBETH

I know!

LADY

Still he's pretty reliable.

MACBETH

Is he?

LADY

Well if he's not I wish you'd find someone else to shepherd our guests in.

MACBETH

Okay, honey, look, I know you're still— we're still— I know things are still— but, y'know, hey, we're [getting better], and if we could— just— on my last night here, if we could maybe not—

                    LADY
Maybe not what?

                    MACBETH
Not do this?

                    LADY
What? Knit? You want me to stop knitting the little [booties?]— are these upsetting you?

                    MACBETH
Are they upsetting *you*?

                    LADY
                (tears brewing)
Why would they upset me?

                    MACBETH
Let's just have a nice night.

                    LADY
                (tears simmering)
I'm having a nice night you're not having a nice night?

                    MACBETH
Honey.

                    LADY
                (tears bubbling)
I'm having a lovely evening.

                    MACBETH
Honey. I'm sorry.

                    LADY
                (actively not crying)
What are you sorry about?

                    MACBETH
I'm sorry about the [baby]
I'm just sorry. I'm really, really sorry.

                    LADY
Me too. It's okay.

LADY (CONT'D)
(an emotional one-eighty)

I love you! I'm fine.

MACBETH

Of course you are!

> *A reassuring smile. She responds, and goes back to knitting.*

Hey. Hey you. It's gonna be a while before /we see each other again—

LADY

Yes it is.

> *Silence.*

MACBETH

It's gonna be kind of like a *long* while before we /see each other again.

LADY
(too close to the last spat, she glares)

Well then *stay home*, Mack, what do you want from me?

> *MACBETH gives a lovely stupid sweet simpering tiny cute baby smile which is endearing and small and very non-threatening and behind which hulks The Idiot, Desire. Beat.*

LADY

I'm knitting.

MACBETH

You're *very* becoming when you knit.

LADY

Uh-huh.

MACBETH

I mean it! I like seeing you with those two long, sharp needles. There's something so
Right. About it.

> *(as if seeing it for the first time, and realizing it is, somehow, the future)*

It's actually kinda... weird, how right... it is.

The two needles drip with red yarn.

LADY

Mack, if you wanna fuck we can fuck, I don't need, like, *coddling*, so just be a *man* and *go for it*, I don't like all this

(sing-song)

"nee-nee-nee-nee" around the subject, and that fucking spider is still there and it's giving me the creeps so just—

She rises to kill the spider.

He rises as well.

MACBETH

Hey now c'mon leave the li'l guy alone

LADY

It's not a "li'l guy" it's a goddamn tarantula

MACBETH

He's not bothering you just let it be

LADY

They bite /and how do you know it's a he?

MACBETH

They *kill vermin* and I just know

LADY

I don't want /to eat it

MACBETH

/You're not gonna eat him

LADY	**MACBETH**
I don't want to have little spider legs wriggling /between my teeth making a web in my guts tangling up my innards and besides it's not a "him" it's a	That is the most preposterous he would probably die in your stomach acids could you just relax

They meet in a passionate kiss over the spider.
Maybe it's been a minute since they had sex.

MACBETH

Don't. Kill him.

LADY

Make me

Kiss.

I'm gonna kill every. Single. Fucking. Insect. While you're gone. Whatcha gonna do about it?

Okay. That's... weird, but like, maybe sort of hot.
He'll take what he can get. He kisses her.

(punctuating her speech with kisses, and drawing
the needle ever closer to his jugular)
I'm gonna kill all the spiders And the flies
I'm gonna spear all those little crawly guys with all the legs that wobble across the wall
I'ma massacre the mice
And all their teeny mice babies.
And when the cat gets jealous of how good I am at killing mice? I'ma kill the cat.
I'll skin the li'l kitty alive and use its whiskers to floss all the spider legs from between my teeth
And when the dog gets suspicious and wonders where the cat went?
I'll poison the pooch.
Nightshade in his meat

MACBETH

Haggis

LADY

he'll go all foamy at the mouth

MACBETH

Haggis

LADY

dead in seconds

MACBETH

Haggis!

She stops kissing him.

LADY	MACBETH
Oh. Oh god I'm sorry did I go too far again? You didn't say /haggis yeah you didn't say the safe word so I kept going.	Haggis.

MACBETH

I'm saying it now.

LADY

Okay but we have the word for, like, *the moment* you're feeling like something's unsafe so if you don't say it until *after* the—

MACBETH

Haggis!

LADY
(realizing the needle is still at his throat)

Oh, oh fuck, I'm sorry I'm so sorry. I hear you. Haggis. Got it. Haggis.
Jesus I am just fucking this up.
Aren't I.

MACBETH

It's— okay, look, I'm trying to be more open to this side of you, because I know there's— stuff— you need to express and— I know we're trying to... reignite... to rekindle our [sex life] because it's been [a while] and I don't want you to feel [rejected], but like... I like our cat.

LADY

Oh god I'm sorry, I don't— I don't *really* wanna kill the cat, it's just a weird— I have all this—

MACBETH

I know, I know, everyone has... kinks, you're fine, you're not weird.

LADY

It's not a kink, it's— I'm— I think I'm really—

MACBETH

You're okay.

LADY

I am?

MACBETH

Yes. Absolutely! Yes! You're okay, I'm okay, we're okay. Okay? Everything's okay.

Let's— why don't we go to bed. Hm? Let's just— we'll just spoon and cuddle. Hm? Yeah?

LADY

Yeah. Yes. Okay. Spoon and cuddle.

MACBETH

C'mon.

A tender embrace.

To bed, to bed, to bed.

They exit.

A moment later, LADY reenters to retrieve her needles. She picks them up. Stares at them. The red yarn dangles and drips. She turns to go when: The Fucking Spider catches her eye. She pauses.

Checks to make sure MACBETH has gone. Considers.

Raises her foot, and:

Squish.

Ecstasy.

(offstage)

Honey?

LADY

Coming!

She exits with purpose.

Lights.

End of play.

Leap Frog

by

Kia Corthron

KIA CORTHRON

For her body of work for the stage, Kia Corthron has been awarded the Windham Campbell Prize, United States Artists Jane Addams Fellowship, Flora Roberts Award, Simon Great Plains Playwright Award, McKnight Fellowship, and others. Plays produced in New York by Playwrights Horizons, New York Theatre Workshop, Ensemble Studio Theatre, Atlantic Theater Company, Manhattan Theatre Club, New York Stage and Film; regionally by the Goodman, Actors Theatre of Louisville, Minneapolis' Children's Theatre, Mark Taper Forum, Hartford Stage, Alabama Shakespeare Festival, Yale Rep, Center Stage, and elsewhere; in London by the Royal Court Theatre and Donmar Warehouse. Her debut novel *The Castle Cross the Magnet Carter* won the 2016 Center for Fiction First Novel Prize and was a *New York Times Book Review* Editor's Choice. TV: *The Jury*, *The Wire*. She serves on the Dramatists Guild Council, is a member of the Authors Guild, and is an alumnus of New Dramatists.

LEAP FROG

appeared in the
2019 Red Bull Theater Short New Play Festival:
The Evil Plays

CAST OF CHARACTERS

S.K. is a black man. He is earnest.

Yuri is a black man. He is a bit self-important, arrogant.

C.O. is an offstage voice.

Setting: A room. The present.
Running Time: Fifteen minutes.

A NOTE FROM THE AUTHOR

Riffing on Aristophanes.

LEAP FROG

Two newspapers held up so as to conceal the faces of their readers. A deck of playing cards on the floor. Suddenly YURI lowers his paper.

YURI

Play!

S.K. more reluctantly lowers his paper, goes to sit with YURI and the cards. The men wear prison garb. S.K. shuffles, offers YURI the deck. YURI plucks from the top.

(reads:)

"Jealousy."

(considers)

Pass.

As S.K. thinks, YURI writes "JEALOUSY" on a small blackboard or whiteboard, displaying it for the players— and the audience— to see.

S.K.

1857: D.C. D.A. Philip Barton Key, son of Francis Scott, begins renting a house from a quote "colored" man to dick around with Teresa, wife of Congressman Dan Sickles, an incorrigible dickaround himself. When in 1859 Sickles finally gets wind of what everyone else in Washington knows, he aims his pistol. Unarmed Key begs for his life, throwing his opera glasses at Sickles, as Sickles shoots Key several times till dead in full daylight, full view of Washingtonian elite society. Sickles makes history as the first American to plead temporary insanity and, after an hour's deliberation, the jury acquits.

YURI

(considers what S.K. has said, thinks; then:)

2013, Saudi Arabia: Man divorces his wife after seeing a photo of her kissing someone else on social media. The someone else was a horse. The wife was not regretful, saying she loved Arabian horses. It should be noted she was falsely accused: she and the horse were just friends.

S.K.

(considers; then confident:)

China, 2015. Man uses his wife's phone to send a sexty email to his lover and forgets to log out. Wife sees message. While Husband sleeps, Wife chops off penis. Husband goes to the hospital, has the thing surgically reattached.

S.K. (CONT'D)

Then Wife goes to the hospital, finds Husband and chops the thing off again, flinging it out the window. This time, with the likely collaboration of feral dogs, the item in question is never recovered.

YURI
(considers; then:)

Leap.

> YURI turns around, and S.K., victorious, leap-frogs Yuri. It should be child's play, not sexual.

Pluck.

S.K.
(plucks next card, reads:)

"Narcissism."

(considers)

Play.

YURI
(erasing "JEALOUSY" and writing "NARCISSISM" on the board)

Narcissus is obviously disqualified.

S.K.

Kanye West.

YURI

Also obvious.

S.K.

His album *Yeezus* features the song "I Am a God." Stopped a concert in Sydney to demand everybody stand, singled out two audience members who didn't, the rest of the audience booed them. Turns out, they *couldn't* stand. Disabled.

YURI
(thinks, then:)

The Egyptian Pharaohs Khufu, Khafre and Menkaure of the Fourth Dynasty. Balance their three pyramid tombs atop one another and the tower would rise above Chicago's John Hancock skyscraper.

S.K.
(thinks)

Can we go political?

                    YURI
Open game, but Pol Pot and Hitler lose points for lack of imagination.

                    S.K. starts to speak.

And Trump.

                    S.K. closes his mouth.

                    S.K.
                    (thinks, light bulb:)
Picasso. His immeasurable ego and arrogance drove a wife, lover, and grandson to suicide, his son drinking himself to death. "Women are machines for suffering," he told a mistress. Decades before Kanye, Pablo proclaims, "I am God."

                    YURI
                    (impressed, then a new idea, smiles:)
Scientologists.

                    S.K. looks at YURI, sighs, bends over. Yuri leap-frogs over S.K.

                    YURI
                    (draws a card, reads:)
"Greed."

                    (thinks)
Pass.

                    Erases the board, writes.

                    S.K.
The Menendez Brothers, rich boys murdered their own parents for the—

                    YURI
The opposite of greed is generosity, and I will *generously* give you a second chance to be more original.

                    S.K.
                    (embarrassed, thinks; then:)
Bhopal.

                    YURI
                    (nods, impressed; then his own turn:)
Exxon deceiving the public about climate change.

S.K.

Fifteen thousand dead after a Union Carbide, now Dow Chemical, accident releases *thirty tons* of poisonous gases into Bhopal, India. That doesn't count the thousands blinded, thousands of birth defects, animal carcasses, all preventable had Union Carbide now Dow Chemical met its own plant safety standards, if Indian officials had bothered looking into worker complaints that were warnings but *that* might have cost Carbide now Dow a nickel or two, *greed!*

YURI

Exxon's own scientists cry climate change back in '77 so Exxon proceeds to cover up the data, to *lie* about the data, denies the facts for profit putting the entire world, repeat entire *world* at risk.

A glaring standoff. Then:

S.K.

The U.S. makes up five percent of the world's population but, thanks to the greed of private prison profiteers, *twenty-five* percent of the world's *prisoner* population.

Pause. Then YURI leans over and S.K. leaps over him. S.K. plucks.

(reads:)
"Competitiveness."

YURI
(frowns)
"Competitiveness"?

Takes the card, reads it himself. Then rips it in two.

S.K.

Hey!

YURI

Isn't this the Deck of Evil? Who says competition's evil?

S.K.

We were just talking about corporate greed, Yuri! What are corporations but competitive?

YURI

It's the *greed* that's evil, not the competition, I would argue, *Mr. Liss*, I would argue that playing that card would lead us down a path of ambiguity, of irreconcilable arbitration. Monopoly— mergers and concentration of business, of media— *that's* the direct path to greed. Competitiveness is the *antidote* to monopoly. Competition urges one to be one's best self, encourages great productivity, great achievement. Competition is Aeschylus and Euripides playing the dozens in Hades to a frog chorus, competition is *you*, S.K., and *me* in *this* Hades playing to stay sane, I would contend that—

S.K.

All right, all right!

(plucks, reads:)

"Blind obedience."

(thinks)

Play.

YURI

(as he erases and writes:)

Again I would advise against the swastika-conspicuous.

S.K.

(smiles)

Jim Jones.

(correction:)

The *followers* of Jim Jones!

YURI

Why?

S.K.

Why?

YURI stares.

For drinking the kool-aid!

YURI makes a buzzer "Wrong!" sound.

What!

YURI

Drinking the Kool-aid wasn't blind obedience, it was duress. Jones's good soldiers focused their semiautomatics on the flock, the people were *forced* to drink the Kool-aid, or more likely its competitor Flavor-Aid, probably praying the drink *might* not kill them in the way the AK-47 surely would, Guyana was not mass suicide, it was mass *murder*.

S.K.

Well... Then the good soldiers *targeting* the flock—

YURI

No after-edits. 2013: A female resident—

S.K.

Wait! I lose that hand?

YURI

I still have to play. If you deem my contribution legit, I leap. If not, this hand is a draw.

S.K.

The *last* hand—

YURI

The *last* hand was a pass. In 2013, a female resident of a southern California retirement home stops breathing. A staff nurse calls 911. The 911 dispatcher tries in myriad ways to get the nurse to perform CPR on the woman but the nurse refuses. The desperate dispatcher then begs the nurse to ask some bystander to help the woman, time is of the essence. The nurse seems remotely shaken but stands her ground: with such an incident she is obligated to call 911 but it's *against company policy*

> *(pointing to the board for emphasis)*

for the nurse to in any way actually *help* the woman. By the time EMT arrives, the woman is dead.

> *Beat. Then S.K. bends over, and YURI leaps. Yuri plucks.*

YURI
> *(reads:)*

"Hypocrisy."

> *(considers)*

Play.

S.K. erases, writes.

YURI (CONT'D)

In 1974 The Charles Koch Foundation, soon re-christened The Cato Institute, is established by Koch as a libertarian think tank espousing, among various policy positions, the privatization or abolishment of social security. A year before, when Koch invited a renowned Austrian libertarian economist to work for him, the scholar declined the offer due to health issues, preferring to stay in his home country where healthcare was free. Though billionaire Koch easily could have paid the man's hospital bills, he instead wrote a letter to the scholar detailing how he could apply for American social security in order to obtain affordable health care.

S.K.

Okay! Since *you* opened the door to political...

(chuckles ironic)

Where to start? In 2014, Trump tweets "with all of the problems and difficulties facing the U.S., President Obama spent the day playing golf." Two and a half years into his presidency, Trump had been on the golf course, one of his *own* golf courses, a hundred and eighty-eight times. President Trump rails against what he calls "chain migration," American citizens accessing citizenship for foreign relatives, while allowing the First Lady's Slovenian parents to attain U.S. citizenship by precisely that method, *Iran!* Obama works out a nuclear deal—

YURI

Pick one.

S.K.

(thinks: hard to decide!)

Iran. After the Obama administration and the *world* come to an agreement, a negotiated *peace*, in comes Trump with his provocative sanctions claiming *they're* for peace, *then* pumped up by Bolton in his cabinet and Netanyahu in *his* Knesset, *warmongers* egging on regime change—

YURI

Venezuela.

S.K.

(beat)

Huh?

YURI

Trump pushing for regime change in Iran just like the U.S. pushing for regime change in Venezuela.

S.K.

Yes. Yeah, well. Maduro is hardly—

YURI

A team of one hundred international observers give the Venezuelan election proceedings its highest ratings. They send a letter to the European Union to chastise it for its disgraceful fabrications delegitimizing the election, Maduro may not be a sweetheart but for all our bewailing Venezuelan suffering, we've done nothing to ease the harsh U.S. sanctions which *cause* plenty of the suffering, sanctions sanctioned by establishment Democrats in partnership with Republicans, both sides vying for the self-exiled Venezuelan Floridian vote come 2020. The elite Dems who cry foul regarding possible Russian interference in *our* elections and in the same breath demand to screw around with *Venezuela's*, hypocrisy.

> *They stare at each other.*

S.K.

Deadlock.

YURI
(chuckles derisively)

If you say so.

S.K.
(glares; plucks; reads:)

"Cruelty."

> *The word silences them both to melancholic
> contemplation.*

Play.

> *YURI erases, writes.*

Child separation at the border. Tearing babies from their mothers' breasts, nothing new in America. Slavery.

YURI
(nods in solemn agreement)

Slavery.

S.K.

The children *still* separated, some maybe *never* reunited with their parents, children *dying* in U.S. custody! How many so far? Six? Border patrol pouring out jugs of water people left for people crossing the desert, the *corpses* in the desert…

Shakes his head in despair.

YURI

Abu Ghraib. Bagram. Guantánamo, black sites of torture, in Guantánamo 780 men and boys detained with no due process, 86 percent seized when the U.S. had the brilliant idea of offering five-thousand-dollar-per-man bounties to poor countries, oh *that* shouldn't lead to any false arrests. Over the course of the prison's **17**-year history almost all detainees were gradually cleared with no charges ever filed, some of whom died before they were freed. Forty remain with five cleared for release but the Trump administration has shown no interest in releasing them.

S.K.

Chelsea Manning. The Espionage Act was a hundred-year-old barely used statute created to prosecute spies but resurrected in the 21st century to actively and aggressively target journalists and their insider informants—

YURI

Resurrected by the *Obama* administration

S.K., an Obama supporter, is irritated.

and when things started getting out of control, Obama started backing off but too late: the monster was unleashed, gift-wrapped for Trump.

S.K.

Manning has the evidence. Video of soldiers firing from a helicopter on civilians including reporters, then firing on a civilian van that stopped to help the victims, killing a father and wounding his children. Manning is accused of slipping the video to WikiLeaks, and instead of being mortified and outraged by the slaughter of civilians, the government and plenty of citizens are mortified and outraged by the *reporting* of the slaughter of civilians—

YURI

You know what?

S.K. sighs hard.

You should have gone with Assange, I would have given you extra points for the controversy factor. Someone accused of rape in Sweden which the U.S. hopes to use to bring him here, lock him up and shut WikiLeaks down, the feds dreaming that a *sexual assault* crime could be leveraged to allow the U.S. to go unscrutinized in its *war* crimes, oh yeah! The feds suddenly are very concerned about violence against women.

S.K.

But instead of being mortified and outraged by the slaughter of civilians, we are mortified and outraged by the *reporting* of the slaughter of civilians, claiming a risk to national security—

YURI
(laughs)

"Risk to national security," *anything* can be deemed "a risk to national security" if it's a risk to national embarrassment, national *shame, wait.* Upright moral Americans just buying the government line to justify American war atrocities, I see where you're headed but that's *hypocrisy, blind obedience,* we're past those, the card in play is *cruelty.* There's overlap, but I really don't believe Manning—

S.K.

WILL YOU LET ME FINISH?

YURI

But! If you're going that route—

S.K. scream-groans.

C.O.
(off:)

QUIET!

Quiet.

YURI

If you're going that route,

S.K. sighs

I'd've given you credit if you hadn't made the obvious choice, if you'd picked, say, Jeffrey Sterling. Do you know Jeffrey Sterling? Former CIA agent, a rare *black* insider who files a racial discrimination lawsuit against the CIA which is thrown out of court because the court claims presenting evidence of racism in the CIA would be a risk to national security. Years later, after being accused of leaking sensitive documents about a dubious CIA plan to a *New York Times* reporter, Sterling is one of the few whistleblowers convicted and actually sentenced to prison time, the CIA does not forget.

(pause)

Your turn.

S.K.

Uninterrupted?

YURI locks his lips and throws away the key. Beat.

S.K. (CONT'D)

Chelsea Manning. Imprisoned after releasing video evidence of U.S. war crimes in Iraq, serves seven years till 2017, two in solitary confinement, then recently back to jail again: two months, one in solitary, then back to jail... Excessive segregation leads to madness, yet once Manning was placed in seg as *punishment* for a suicide attempt, Kalief Browder. Sixteen-year-old black kid accused of stealing a backpack a *backpack—* three years Rikers *awaiting trial,* he was *never tried.* Two of those three years in solitary, his case finally dismissed for lack of evidence freeing his body but not his mind, hanged himself outside his mother's home age twenty-two *Albert Woodfox!* Twenty-five years old, convicted for armed robbery and sentenced to *fifty* years Angola Prison. Becomes a politicized Panther and he and a couple others organize for prisoner rights and after a couple Angola C.O.s wind up dead with nothing tying the Angola Three to the murders, the Angola Three are held responsible Albert Woodfox *forty-three years solitary confinement* MADNESS MADNESS CRUEL!

(pause)

But not so unusual.

Pause.

YURI

Like you. Ten years cocaine possession, but then you get all your colleagues organized complaining about the beatings, complaining about prisoner slavery, about excessive segregation and suddenly here you are: alone. Coming up on, what? Thirteen / years?

S.K.
(chiming in at the slash:)

Thirteen years.

YURI gazes at S.K. Then Yuri bends over for S.K. to leap. S.K. may or may not notice this, and if he does, he will not have yet decided whether to leap before:

C.O.
(off:)

S.K. LISS!

S.K. and YURI turn to the voice. A slot at the back of the room opens— the audience may or may not have noticed it before— and a tray of food pushes through. As S.K. moves toward the tray, Yuri picks up the playing cards, his newspaper, the writing board and writing utensils, and exits.

*When S.K. turns back around, he is startled and a bit
devastated to see YURI is gone. S.K. slowly brings
the tray to where the deck of cards had been, sits.
The food is slop. S.K. takes an unsatisfying bite.
Looks around. Empty. Alone.*

End of play.

The Burning of Bone

by

Marcus Gardley

MARCUS GARDLEY

Marcus Gardley is an acclaimed poet-playwright-screenwriter whom The New Yorker describes as "the heir to Garcia Lorca, Pirandello and Tennessee Williams." In 2019, he was named the Library Laureate of San Francisco by the city's mayor and the recipient of the 2019 Doris Duke Artist Award. He is the recipient of the 2015 Glickman Award, a finalist for the 2015 Kennedy Prize, and a 2019 Obie Award winner for his play *The House That Will Not Stand*. Other plays include *X or the Nation v Betty Shabazz, black odyssey, The Gospel of Living Kindness, Every Tongue, On the Levee,* and *The Road Weeps, The Well Runs Dry*. He is an Artistic Associate for The Young Vic in London. In TV, Marcus has written for several series including Boots Riley's *I'm a Virgo* (Amazon), *The Chi* (Showtime), *Foundation* (Apple), *NOS4A2* (AMC), *Maid, Tales of the City,* and *Mindhunter* (Netflix). He has also developed pilots for HBO. His feature adaptation of *The Color Purple* musical will be released in theatres in December 2023.

THE BURNING OF BONE
appeared in the
2019 Red Bull Theater Short New Play Festival:
The Evil Plays

CAST OF CHARACTERS

Dozens. age unknown, her indentured servant.

Nova. a Griot, age unknown, Dozens' wife

Setting: A plantation, 1676.
Running Time: Ten minutes.

A NOTE FROM THE AUTHOR

1676: A slave rebellion in Virginia. Black and white slaves burned Jamestown to the ground. Hundreds died. The planters feared a reoccurrence. They divided the races against each other. They instilled a sense of superiority in the white slaves and degraded the black slaves. White slaves were given new rights. White slaves whose daily condition was no different from that of Blacks, were taught that they belonged to a superior people.

THE BURNING OF BONE

On the eve of when slavery was legalized in the United States. NOVA GOODE, age unknown, out of breath, runs onto the back porch and stops before her husband, DOZENS, age also unknown, who sits on a stool shelling peas. It is 1676. It is hot.

NOVA

I have some news to tell you, my husband. But I'm afraid it just might kill you.

DOZENS

Then don't tell me.

NOVA

But I must. I must get this off my chest before it breaks my heart into pieces.

DOZENS

Then be quick about it, wife. I'm old. I don't have enough years left on my life to sit through one of your prologues so get to the plot.

NOVA

I can't just spit it out like a loose tooth. This news is heavy. I'm going to need to sit somewhere so I can get this weight off my back.

She waits for him to give up his seat, he does.

DOZENS

I thought you said it was on your chest, now it's on your back too? Sounds like it be everywhere but coming out of your mouth—

NOVA

—Do not start on me this morning, Dozens Goode—

DOZENS

—I wouldn't have to start on you if you started telling your story. /Ain't you supposed to be a Griot? What kind of Griot can't tell a story?

NOVA

/I'll tell it when I gets ready to tell it! I don't tell you how to tell your tacky tall tales. I have to warm up to it—

DOZEN

—It's too hot for you to be warming up! Hurry now and speak!—

NOVA

—THE FIELD HANDS ARE GOING TO REVOLT!!!

DOZENS

Woah. Come again.

NOVA

The field hands: them boys who work in the fields with their hands. They're going to revolt! I overheard them whispering when I was in the tobacco fields this morning.

DOZENS

You mean to say you were eavesdropping on them again.

NOVA

No, I mean to say... I was in the fields when they were easily dropping whispers that drifted into my ear this morning. T'was early: Mother Dawn had already danced over the Red Hills and now she was picking up her sun from the river and lifting his golden face into the sky. Myself: I was walking by the tobacco fields, gathering flowers for the wedding when I overheard them— the field hands. They said they're going to set fire to their master's crops and houses then meet on the main road to form an army and burn Jamestown to the ground. There's going to be a slave revolt, my husband. These Negroes done lost their godforsaken minds—

He moves her away from possible earshot.

DOZENS

—Shhh! Are you sure they said they were going to revolt?

NOVA

They didn't use that word but what else you call it when slaves take up arms, set fire to crops and burn down their master's houses? I wouldn't call it a country picnic, I'd call it a barbecue! I better go to tell the master! He must be warned!—

DOZENS

—Hold your thighs! We can't get involved in this. We're House Negroes. House Negroes are only supposed to tend to matters concerning the house.

NOVA

But they're going to burn down the house. And with us in it.

DOZENS

So! This ain't our house! We were bought by the master to be servants in the house, which means we're here to serve not to protect. We need to just keep quiet, then right before dusk falls we'll run for shelter in the hills. If we tell our master what the field hands are up to, who do you think they're going to put their hands on next?

NOVA

The master would never harm you; you're like a friend to him.

DOZENS

He calls me boy and I'm old. If he a friend, I'd rather work for an enemy.

NOVA

Don't matter, I can't waste no time. I gots to warn him.

She tries to walk off, DOZENS grabs her.

DOZENS

We can't blame them field hands for being angry. They've had enough of tillin', toilin' the land. Even in this red heat, I can feel their rage coming to a boil. Word in the wind say the Virginia Courts are trying to pass a new law legalizing lifetime slavery for all Negro servants. Can you imagine? Forced to be a slave for your entire life when you were told you only had to be an indentured servant for several years! These colonists are getting so rich off of Negro labor that they are even willing to bend laws to feed their fat bellies and England's great mouth. Apparently, the courts will pass this law in three days if somebody doesn't fight back. If folks don't demand their rights as human persons, they'll build their kingdom with our bones and raise their homes on our very backs.

NOVA

Mercy. Just listen to yourself. If I didn't know you any better, I'd assumed you'd had joined the revolt yourself, my husband.

(beat)

My husband, have you joined the revolt yourself?

DOZENS

Sometimes a man has to follow his own convictions—

NOVA

—Oh, Lord of mercy! Have you lost your mind! /They're going to kill you. They're going to kill me!

DOZENS

/A man has to do his part so others will look in the annals of history and know, that somebody stood against tyranny. They are an evil, wife! I know you've been reading that good book they gave you and it says servants obey your masters but that commandment itself is evil. No man nor woman should belong to any man or woman. Every heart knows it's wrong so why do we allow our minds to accept it? Just 'cause we live in the house don't mean we treated like children of God. We just as damned if we don't fight. It's time we took a stand!

NOVA

But I'm your good woman. How can you stand anywhere without me by your side? How can you even stand for long? Don't you got two trick knees?

DOZENS

I'm standing on the memory of where we come from! This not our land, wife. These colonists spilled the blood of other men to sow this land, then brought us here so our sweat and tears could water and seed it, so that they can grow futures for their children. We will never find peace here.

NOVA

We will as long as we get our piece.

DOZENS

But ain't you worth more?!

He tries to touch her, she recoils.

I never told you I had joined the revolution 'cause it's too dangerous for you to be by my side. That's why I keep you in here: in my heart. I'm your husband and a husband's duty is to protect his wife. I'm protecting you sugar lumpkin—

He tries to kiss her neck, she moves.

NOVA

—Keep you're lump of sugar, I need you to be alive. We'll be free in a few months. We'll have worked off the years we owe in servitude. We just need to be patient.

DOZENS

—Woman, ain't you listening? They're taking our freedoms. In a few months, we'll no longer be indentured— we'll be slaves and old slaves at that. The time to act is now. We're going to do it tonight right before dusk when the master goes to bed, we're going to set fire to the white house. We're going to burn down the master's house with him still inside. Then we'll meet on the main road, march into Jamestown and burn the courthouse to the ground.

NOVA

This is madness, I don't even know who you are anymore. What have you done to my real huz. Is he even still inside you?

DOZENS

Look me in mine eyes, you know who I am. Who I've always been. I ain't never been one to keep my head bowed or keep quiet when others are wronged. The worst thing a group of folks can be when they are being governed by evil is to stay quiet. Quiet is the loudest way to tell the master that he can treat you and others like dirt. When will enough be enough, my wife? Our sons are living in threat of the law, shot at for merely walking home at night. Our children are brought here in cages and our women raped without recourse. We must stand up for ourselves or this evil will be allowed to continue into generations. We must burn down the house.

NOVA

The master is still a child of God. He do evil but he just a man. And the people love him some. He good as far as master's go. He don't work us too hard, lets us eat the meat off the bone and gives us Sundays off to pray to our God.

DOZENS

His God.

NOVA

It's God nevertheless. Even if you kill this master, you got to know there's just going to be another that come behind him and then another and yet and still another behind that one. We don't live in the only white house in this country. Every house is white. Almost every son of the master is raised to believe that he can keep his heel on our necks. You can't burn that thinking out of folks. It's in their bones. We will never have true freedom in this country. The land is already cursed. Only choice we have is to work hard, hope to get our freedom, our piece of property and live off that till we die.

DOZENS

That ain't no life though, wife! What we are living IS NOT A LIFE! LOOK 'ROUND! Every day we're turnin' our backs and closing our eyes to the sins these men commit on the innocent. It ain't enough to whisper curses or call them devil behind their backs. Men must ACT! Ain't it better to die fighting for what's right than to live a long life when you know you're wronged?

NOVA

We will always be wronged. This is what I'm trying to tell you. This vision for a bright future you done gave yourself is makin' you blind. You can't burn what's in men's bones. What's in their nature. Most men don't change— they ain't like the seasons. Their nature is to grow against nature.

DOZENS

Then we must rid them all till it's a new day.

DOZENS starts to head off. She stops him.

NOVA

—Mercy!! You sound dumb-found. Sit down. It must be the heat. Come, sit. Let me fix you a cool glass of water and I shall wash your thoughts of this. I won't lose you.

She starts to weep. He grabs her softly. ACTORS make sounds off stage: the sea and winds. DOZENS rocks NOVA in his arms.

DOZENS

This, touchin' you reminds me of the first time we met. 'Member. I was asleep on the bottom floor of that vessel when it went swaying to and fro. Them sailors had brought you below, shackled at the wrist and ankle. And threw you next to me. A seaman had tried to put his hands on you and you nearly bit off his pecker. So they beat you halfway into death. You was real sickly when they dropped you by my side. I saw you for the first time. 'Member. Half-naked, bloody, bruised and yet oh so beautiful. So beautiful in fact that I could no longer sleep. We were packed in tight and that night, I managed to get a hand free. Broke my wrist so I could hold you. I held you. Watched over you till you woke. Fed you my slop, cooled you from the wind of my breath. Cleaned your nose, licked your blood and held your body close when you screamed in your dreams. You tried to leave me alone in this world but I made you fight death. I sung you my mother's song. 'Member.

NOVA
(singing very slowly)
/Thula thul', thula baba,
thula sana,
Thul' ubab' uzofika,
ekuseni. [repeat]

DOZENS

I begged you to hang on. I said there
was so much life left. You didn't
know me from a roach on the wall
but you held onto my free hand,
never said a word to me for days,
never even looked me in the eyes...
but you lived.

DOZENS (CONT'D)

You thought I saved your life but in truth, wife. I had decided to jump overboard next time they brought me up to the deck. It was you, who gave me a reason to carry on. And you have done so everyday. I have to fight. I will fight, my love. I will do it for you. It's the only way to make sure we are not slaves for the remainder of our lives. And I implore you. Do not mention a word of this to our master. Do not betray your husband.

NOVA

But you know I can't keep a secret to save my life—

She tries to break free but he grabs her.

DOZENS

—Look at me! You will keep this secret. In your good book it say a wife's duty is to serve her husband. If you can serve this house for thirteen years, I believe this one time you can find it in your heart to serve me.

He lets her go.

NOVA

You're a fool for following those field hands. The law is going to hang you, husband!

DOZENS

Who says I'm a follower. Look at me good, my wife. Your husband is the leader!

This news hits her like lightning. She stands frozen. He kisses her head and walks off, leaving her to stare at us as lights fade to black.

End of play.

Pardon My Greed!

by

Terry Glaser

TERRY GLASER

Terry Glaser is a playwright, translator, stage director, actor, and acting teacher. Her writing includes translations and adaptations of classic plays and operas, including *The Frogs* (Aristophanes), *A Flea in Her Ear* (Feydeau), *The Surprise of Love* (Marivaux), *Croquefer* (Offenbach), and *Orfeo* (Monteverdi). Her original dramatic works include *Love-Blooded,* a tragicomedy about the Trojan War, which was named a Semi-finalist in the 2021 Shakespeare's New Contemporaries Competition at the American Shakespeare Center; the Commedia dell'Arte farce *The Dentist*; and solo shows in which she performs the life stories of playwrights, including *The Mysterious Dwarf* (Gogol), and *Chekhov, Live!* (Chekhov). Ms. Glaser has been stage director for over 50 professional and university productions across the country, has performed her solo shows and conducted master classes at universities nationwide, and has served on the Theatre and Music faculties of the University of Southern California, the University of San Diego, CalArts, and the University of California San Diego. Ms. Glaser holds a B.A. in Playwriting from Brown University and an M.A. in Theatre from Syracuse University.

PARDON MY GREED!
appeared in the
2019 Red Bull Theater Short New Play Festival:
The Evil Plays

CAST OF CHARACTERS

Chaucer. The poet.

Pardoner. A person authorized, through the sale of indulgences, to grant remission from punishment for sins.

Merek. A wastrel.

Carac. A wastrel.

Brom. A wastrel.

Priest. A clergyman.*

Old Man. An elderly pauper.*

These two roles can be played by the same actor and can be cast gender-neutral.

Setting: The floor of the stage is painted to represent a meandering dirt road, with the audience seated alongside the road, and a wooden table and chair at one end of the road. The time is the Middle Ages in England.

Running Time: Approximately ten minutes.

A NOTE FROM THE AUTHOR

Based on a tale from Chaucer's *The Canterbury Tales*, *Pardon My Greed!* fuses the past and the present in an all-too-familiar story of avarice, political corruption, and the hope for a better life to come.

PARDON MY GREED!

SETTING: The floor of the stage is painted to represent a meandering dirt road. The audience is seated alongside the road. In neutral clothing, all the ACTORS except for CHAUCER are sitting among the audience. When characters enter the story, acting out what CHAUCER or the PARDONER describes, the ACTORS put on an appropriate costume piece and jump up from the audience, returning to it when they have finished their scene. At one end of the road are a wooden table and chair.

AT RISE: The stage is dark. In the darkness, we hear the sound of rain. A small pool of light, as if coming from a candle, comes up on a man in a long robe seated at the table, which is covered with sheets of parchment, an inkwell, pens, and the candle. The man is writing.

        CHAUCER
      (reading what he has just written)
Whan that Aprille with his shoures sote
The droghte of Marche hath perced to the rote,

      (to the audience)
I think you'll find it needs no more explaining
To simply say it's spring and that it's raining.
And when the leaden sky is streaming tears,
Repentance for the sins of reckless years
Demands heartfelt atonement for what's owed,
And makes of man a pilgrim on the road.
Plain English? When the heavens start to drip,
Good sinners know it's time to take a trip.
So I, one year, unshriven, full of rue,
Was moved to make a journey, and, like you,
I found myself upon the path to grace,
And there did meet all kinds of men— debased,
Corrupt, and foul— by Lucifer enslaved—
On pilgrimage and wanting to be saved
From hellfire, their reward for doing evil.
Salvation's full of pain— how medieval!
And what is evil's source, its root and seed?

PARDONER

Well, I can tell you that— the culprit's greed.

CHAUCER

The Pardoner was one I met, and he
Would save your sinful soul, but for a fee.

PARDONER

We're talking greed, we're talking gluttony. We're talking gluttony, we're talking intemperance. Intemperance— I'll drink to that!

> *He takes a flagon out of the large bag he's wearing and takes a hefty swig.*

Radix malorum est cupiditas.

CHAUCER

He speaks the truth— *in vino veritas.*
Rapacity, voracity, avidity, and lust.
It takes an expert to engender trust.

PARDONER

And let's throw in a pie for good measure.

> *He wolfs down a pie.*

See, here's how it works. I got this great arrangement with the Church. It's my job to scare the hell out of you with stories of how if you do even one eensy teensy little thing wrong during the miserable moth-eaten existence we call life on earth, instead of spending eternity lounging on a cloud of soft pillows with an unending supply of mead, you'll be cast down into the pit of hell, where hundred-headed demons with reeking breath will sink their venomous teeth into your bowels and grind them up for sausage meat. And that's on a good day. So, anyway, once I've laid out the general scheme of things, I give you this fantastic way out: an indulgence.

> *He whips out a piece of paper from his sack.*

One measly scrap of stinking goatskin and your soul's washed clean as a newborn lamb. Everyone's a sinner, my friends, but you, too, can be the proud new owner of a pristine soul. Step right up, lords and ladies, peasants and serfs, and get yourself an indulgence— signed by a bishop, signed by a patriarch, even signed by the Pope. And all it costs is a single, solitary groat. Four paltry little pennies, one-third of a shilling, and the skids to eternal bliss are greased like the back end of a Sodomite. Your complete satisfaction is guaranteed. In other words, if you end up at the stake, a sizzling pile of smoldering ash despite the piece of parchment, you get your money back.

CHAUCER

Indulgences should only be remission
Of punishment for mortal sin's commission.
But salvation's what the Pardoner avouches
So simple folk will empty out their pouches.

PARDONER

And, friends, that's not all I got. I got relics. Gen-u-ine, bona fide relics. Be the first on your fief to take home the holy body part of your dreams. Just take a look at these red-hot babies.

He upends his sack and several items fall out.

Here you got the shoulder bone of a sheep, given to me by a converted Jew on his way back from Jerusalem. Dip it in your well— the bone that is, not the Jew— and watch your cattle's maggots wither right away.

CHAUCER

It's nothing but some sanctified hearsay.

PARDONER

And then there's Saint Teresa's crop-increasing mitten.

CHAUCER

The greasy membrane from a still-born kitten.

PARDONER

Saint Peter's brain, the fount of holy power.

CHAUCER

Looks like a head of moldy cauliflower.

PARDONER

All right, wise guy, don't take my word for it. I got witnesses. "The Dangers of Greed: A Morality Play in Four Really Quick Acts." Act 1, A Tavern. Three wastrels: Merek, Carac, and Brom.

MEREK

Let's dance a jig!

CARAC

Let's fuck a pig!

BROM

Let's gamble and whore and drink ourselves sick!

MEREK, CARAC & BROM
(dancing, drinking, and carousing)

More! More! Bring on the stuff!
By the blood of Christ, I can't get enough!

PARDONER

So the three wastrels are cursing and dicing and wenching, swigging ale and cramming meat pies down their gullets, when all of a sudden they hear the pealing of a bell and a voice like the crack of doom.

PRIEST

Ding dong, ding dong. Make way. Corpse coming through. Fresh as a daisy and riddled with sores. Make way for the corpse. Ding dong, ding dong.

MEREK

Hey, brother, who's in the sack?

PRIEST

Churl by the name of Fendrel.

CARAC

Fendrel! Why, he was our pal. We were raping and pillaging together just the other day.

PRIEST

Don't blame me. Death's been on plague duty.

BROM

Poor Fendrel! I say we find this Death fellow and teach him a lesson! Are you with me, friends?

PARDONER

And so, despite the fact that Death had been having a field day, rampaging over the land, mowing down everyone in his path without regard to age or station or worldly goods— despite the fact that the Grim Reaper is nobody to fool around with— our three wastrels swear an oath to be true to each other, find Death, and kill him.

MEREK, CARAC & BROM

One for all and all for one,
We won't give up 'til Death is done!

PARDONER

No sooner do they set out on their valiant quest than they meet a poor old man, all wrapped in rags and tatters.

OLD MAN

God be with you, good sirs.

MEREK

Say, old man, isn't it time you found yourself an unused shroud?

OLD MAN

Believe me, my sons, I've tried, but not even Death will take my weary bones.

CARAC

Did he just say the magic word?

OLD MAN

All I said was that not even—

MEREK, CARAC & BROM

Death!

MEREK

You're in league with Death!

BROM

Sorry, friend, but that was the magic word.

MEREK

And if you don't tell us where Death is hiding, we'll run you through like a piece of rancid meat.

OLD MAN

I don't know why you're in such a hurry. Death will find you sooner or later. But if you really can't wait for Death, check under the oak tree around the corner. That's where I saw him last.

PARDONER

And the old man hobbles away as fast as his shriveled shanks can carry him. The three wastrels go tearing around the corner to the oak tree—

MEREK, CARAC & BROM

This one's for Fendrel!

PARDONER

And come to a screeching halt.

MEREK

Well, will you look at that— an enormous pile of golden coins!

CARAC

And not a soul in sight.

BROM

Not even—

MEREK, CARAC & BROM

Death!

MEREK

Anybody here see Death?

CARAC

Nope.

BROM

Not me.

PARDONER

And they forget all about Death and fall on the pile of gold like a pack of ravenous beasts.

MEREK

All right, brothers, let's get organized. According to the law of finders-keepers, this gold belongs to us. But we can't carry it home by daylight lest we be accused of theft.

BROM

So, what do we do?

CARAC

We carry it home after dark, you idiot.

MEREK

I'll break this stick in three, and whoever draws the shortest piece shall run into town and bring back bread and wine to sustain us. The other two will stay and guard the treasure, and when night falls, we'll take the treasure home, divide it equally amongst ourselves, and live like kings for the rest of our lives.

MEREK breaks a stick into two long pieces and one short one. He holds the short piece out to BROM.

MEREK

Here, Brom, you draw first.

BROM

But—

MEREK

Right. That's settled. See you tonight, brother.

PARDONER

And Brom runs off. Meanwhile, Merek and Carac hatch a plot to stab Brom when he returns and thus get bigger shares of the gold. At the same time, Brom cooks up a scheme to slip deadly nightshade into his friends' wine and keep all the gold for himself. So when Brom returns—

CHAUCER

Your time is up, I can't sit here all day.
Let's have the denouement without delay.

PARDONER
(speaking very quickly)

Act 2: Wastrels One and Two stab Wastrel Three. Act 3: Wastrel Three, before he gives up the ghost, offers Wastrels One and Two the secretly poisoned wine as a token of his forgiveness. Act 4: Wastrels One and Two, not wanting to appear ungrateful, drink the wine and die an agonizing death. So, the three wastrels, cursèd sinners that they are, reap the just rewards of their avarice and are cast down into the pit of hell, where hundred-headed demons with reeking breath sink their venomous teeth into their bowels and grind them up for sausage meat.

CHAUCER

The wastrels, full of avarice and greed,
Evil through and through in thought and deed,
Earned everlasting torment for their pact—
Is this the moral in the final act?

PARDONER

The moral is: get yourself some fire insurance. This is what I preach from the pulpit. I stand there just like a priest and warn the ignorant ninnyhammers in the congregation that if they don't forsake the sin of avarice and practice the virtue of charity— especially to me— they'll be cast down into the pit of—

CHAUCER

We know this bit, we've learned it all by heart,
Just tell us what's the secret of your art.

PARDONER
(laughing uproariously)

Secret? Art? That's a laugh! It's all perfectly straightforward. I'm lying through my teeth. And I make no bones about it. I'm a cheat, a charlatan, a cozener, and a crook. And if you don't believe me, just ask the hundreds of gullible addlepates who fork over their hard-earned pennies in the belief that their sins will be forgiven only to find themselves wallowing in a bog of boiling brimstone until the end of time. But that's not my problem. Once they're dead, it's none of my business. I don't care about their souls, all I want is their money. See, the trick is to practice what you preach. I preach against greed, and then I practice it! What could be more convincing?! So I say to you, you're all sinners— treacherous, lecherous, blasphemous malefactors, enmeshed in the trammels of greed and gluttony, and mired in a morass of evil, and if you don't fill my purse with silver, you know the horrible fate that awaits you. Would I lie to you? Of course I would! But you'll bite anyway, because who wants to take a chance when eternity's at stake? So step right up, lords and ladies, peasants and serfs— buy your way into Heaven. And may Christ have mercy on your soul— because sure as God made man in his image, nobody else will.

> *Through CHAUCER'S final speech, the PARDONER mimes hawking his wares as the ACTORS— in dumbshow— crowd around him to buy the indulgences and relics.*

CHAUCER

O tempter— cunning, slippery, and shrewd!
Cajolery that cannot be eschewed!
For would you not believe a canny liar
Who promises salvation from hell's fire
Through purchase of a papal dispensation
Than live a life of pain and abnegation?
Now some may think my tale a flight of fancy
Because I am a poet, but God grant he
Flourishes who heeds my artful preacher,
For fiction will e'er prove the wisest teacher.
This world is but a thoroughfare of woe,
And pilgrims all, we're passing to and fro.
God gave people humor for a reason:
To help them navigate through every season.
So if you cannot laugh through life's chagrin,

CHAUCER (CONT'D)

This rejection of God's gift's another sin.
Now fare you well, I bid you all good night.
Canterbury calls, and I have tales to write.

> *CHAUCER goes back to his writing and the lights fade to black.*
>
> *End of play.*

Something This Way Comes

by

Eric Pfeffinger

ERIC PFEFFINGER

Eric Pfeffinger is a member of the Dramatists Guild and the Writers Guild of America east. His plays have been produced by the Humana Festival of New American Plays at Actors Theatre of Louisville, the Denver Theatre Center, the Geva Theatre Center, the Phoenix Theatre, the InterAct, the 16th Street Theatre, the Source Festival, City Theatre of Miami, the One-Minute Play Festival, and elsewhere. He has written new plays on commissions from the Signature Theatre, the InterAct, Imagination Stage, and the Bloomington Playwrights Project. He's developed new work with PlayPenn, Page 73, the Lark Playwrights Week, the Colorado New Play Summit, the Orlando Shakes PlayFest, HBMG Foundation's Winter Playwrights Retreat, Red Bull, the Purple Rose, Chicago Dramatists, the Rattlestick, Write Now, and others. Eric grew up in Indiana and lives with his family in Toledo, Ohio; he enjoys a robust midwestern humility.

SOMETHING THIS WAY COMES
appeared in the
2019 Red Bull Theater Short New Play Festival:
The Evil Plays

CAST OF CHARACTERS

Lackey. They're a flunky.

Gofer. They're a minion.

Banquo. Banquo is a traveler who's not having the best day.

Setting: *Something This Way Comes* takes place on a remote road, sometime between 1040 and 1606, give or take a day.

Running Time: Ten minutes.

A NOTE FROM THE AUTHOR

It's not often that a play set around the fifteenth century can say it's ripped from the headlines, but that's the vibe *Something This Way Comes* is going for. In performance, the characters are always firmly rooted in their historical moment, except occasionally when they're not. And while the play in its writing had a particular political context in mind, it turns out that deception and venality and selfish rationalizations aren't rare commodities in the realm of public service, rendering Lackey and Gofer's preoccupations regrettably timeless.

SOMETHING THIS WAY COMES

LACKEY and GOFER, waiting. Finally:

LACKEY

Pray, what's the hour?

GOFER

Five minutes hence since last you asked.

LACKEY

I thought to be home ere now. Are we to stand till our feet root in the soil, till the wheels tumble off Phoebus's chariot and the very globe cinders in an icy darkness? Come and say me truly, are we to wait so long?

GOFER

Nay, not that long.

LACKEY

How long, then?

GOFER

Till our business is concluded.

LACKEY

—It's too long.

GOFER

Ay, says thee.

LACKEY

So says any mortal, subject to the natural plagues of time: the gristling of muscle, the grieving of bones. Man's meant not to tarry but to act!

GOFER

Act, then.

LACKEY

Act how?

GOFER

Act like one who minds not waiting.

LACKEY

I'm not so skilled an actor.

GOFER

—'Twill be rain tonight.

LACKEY

And still here we'll stand, like.

GOFER

Let forbearance be your umbrella.

LACKEY

And fury shall be my galoshes, and with them I'll stomp thee into jelly.

GOFER

If thou art so peevish, then go. Just go.

LACKEY

Shall I go?

GOFER

Yes, go.

LACKEY

I shall.

They do not move.

GOFER

...Heard thou about the king?

LACKEY

Go to, what's the newest grief? Each sunrise teems a new one these days.

GOFER

'Tis whispered he seized the throne with bloodied fingers. 'Twas a gift exchange: took he the crown, and in return bestowed upon his predecessor a bodkin to the heart.

LACKEY

Buzz, buzz; this I knew.

GOFER

Fie, I thought I'd grubbed fresh dirt. How know'st thou?

LACKEY

Met some witches magicking in the woods who claim they planted the seeds of his perfidy.

GOFER

Fig's end! The king murders for gain, *and* consorts with occultists?

LACKEY

Even so.

GOFER

'Tis the sort of scuttle could topple a sovereign.

LACKEY

Alas, poor country, it weeps and bleeds.

GOFER
(beat)

Howe'er...

LACKEY

Ay?

GOFER

...His tax plan. It doth please me.

LACKEY

Oh, me as well, 'tis a most fortuitously fashioned levy for mine portfolio. ...But so you're saying, the sorcery, and the murder—

GOFER

I like it not, not one mote.

LACKEY

Nor I. But the *taxes*—?

GOFER

Heigh-ho.

LACKEY
(beat)

What's more though—

GOFER

Ay?

LACKEY

They say also the king spun poisonous fictions, dressing his victim's servants in murderers' clothes. Then he himself slaughtered said servants, feigning righteous rage.

GOFER

—'Tis not *ideal* in a sovereign...

LACKEY

And now 'tis the victim's bereaved sons he's fingered falsely as the killers.

GOFER

Nay.

LACKEY

'Tis so, methinks: the witches said. They had a *cauldron*.

GOFER

So let me say plain: the king's murderous behavior, and the perjury— these things thrill me not. To these I say a hearty nay. Nay, say I!
(beat)
And yet. I must add, on the other hand: the king's taste in jurists. Seems sound.

LACKEY

Verily, he doth appoint capable jurists whose views align with mine own.

GOFER

And forget not the taxes. I ponder how to spend my excess lucre. I may buy a ruff.

LACKEY

'Twould become you.

GOFER

I know it. I've a ruff-friendly nape.

LACKEY

I might fund a holiday to Birnam Wood, if ever we leave this damnèd place.

GOFER

O temper thy haste; Birnam Wood's not going anywhere.

LACKEY

...So, the king, though, see: there's a bit more to't, alack.

GOFER

More calumny about the king? Nay. I credit it not. These, as the maxim goeth, be spurious dispatches.

LACKEY

Marry, the witchy conjurers can pierce Future's veil, and they prophesize... well...

GOFER

More butchery?

LACKEY

Of women. *And* babes. Thieving the property of citizens and marching soldiers to their deaths, all to beshroud his crimes and sentinel his power.

GOFER

Troubling, if so.

LACKEY

O nation miserable. 'Tis wickedness itself.

GOFER

Out upon't, I like not that word.

LACKEY

"Wicked?" Speak'st thou honestly? When our tyrant's a blasphemer more malicious than the damnedest demon in hell, doth evicting the label render his spilling of innocent blood less vile?

GOFER

Just, "wickedness," ugh, alas, the word bears a judgmental burthen, methinks.

LACKEY

What do you prefer?

GOFER

I— "Wickedly tinged?"... 'Tis a work in progress.

LACKEY

Yet on the other *other* hand...

GOFER

More hands hath we than Ganesh by now, methinks...

LACKEY

...Another morsel for the stew: the king swears also he'll accomplish much deregulation.

GOFER

I love deregulation. 'Tis propitious for my trade.

LACKEY

He shall slice through the noxious thickets of officialdom as cleanly as he splits the trunks of innocent children.

GOFER

So in sum: I'm a Yes on the polity that profits me and my like...

LACKEY

I too.

GOFER

But a No on massacres and child-murder...

LACKEY

Strong no.

GOFER

And were I given a vote on the matter...?

LACKEY

(Which is not likely, monarchies being what they are.)

GOFER

I'd really feel I was being asked to venture my predilections on state matters, not so much such character failings as may beset the king at home.

LACKEY

Indeed! 'Tis not that I *endorse* his baseness and bloodied turpitude. I am no avid *supporter* of the mutilation of human beings—

GOFER

Many in my *family* are human beings.

LACKEY

—'tis rather that I *do* approve of these other irrelative matters, which happen to benefit *me*. And being as no man's *perfect*...?

GOFER

O well-spoken fellow, our thoughts be twinned.

LACKEY

—But soft!

GOFER

Hark. Horses. Approaching northerly.

LACKEY

Our wait is lately rewarded, if not timely.

They reveal their weapons.

GOFER

Also to chew upon: were the current king dethroned for someone of godlier disposition? The new ruler likely would not hire us to do these slaughterous jobs.

LACKEY

'Tis true.

GOFER

And what would rampant unemployment among the freelance murtherer class portend for our vibrant economy?

LACKEY

Though the king's a pox on humanity, verily he be a boon to my pockets.

GOFER

Ho! 'Tis them, stand to't.

Enter BANQUO.

                    LACKEY

Hail.

                    GOFER

Hail.

                    BANQUO

What ho, what's this?

                    LACKEY

Villainy, sire.

                    BANQUO

Against who?

                    GOFER

Presently, you.

> LACKEY and GOFER attack. BANQUO struggles and
> falls.

                    BANQUO

Murther! Ho! But why? Tell me— who hast set thee upon me?

                    LACKEY

Your king, knave.

                    BANQUO

The king! Deviltry! O villainy!

                    GOFER

Honestly I love not those words.

                    LACKEY

Also, know this: we liketh his tax plan.

                    BANQUO

As do I. His tax rates profit much my holdings. So with my dying breath I forgive my assassin, for I value his favored treatment of investment income and pass-through earnings. —Also his jurists in my view be largely solid.

                    LACKEY

My heart gladdens: finally, as a nation, we cleave.

They finish murdering.

BANQUO dies.

End of play.

Exposure

by

Bridgette Dutta Portman

BRIDGETTE DUTTA PORTMAN

Bridgette Dutta Portman is a playwright based in Fremont, CA. Dozens of her short plays have been produced locally, across the country, and overseas. Her work was featured in Red Bull Theater's Short New Play Festivals in 2014 and 2016. Her full-length plays include *The Widow of Sisyphus* (semi-finalist, 2011 O'Neill Playwrights' Conference), *La Fee Verte* (Acadiana Repertory Theatre, 2016), *Caeneus & Poseidon* (Dragon Theatre, 2017), *Ageless* (Quantum Dragon Theatre, 2017), and *The Mourner* (Custom Made Theatre, 2018). She has been a finalist for the Bay Area Playwrights' Festival, the PlayPenn Conference, the Garry Marshall New Works Festival, the Kentucky Women's Theatre Conference Prize for Women Writers, and the New Dramatists playwrights' residency. She is past president of the Playwrights' Center of San Francisco, a founding member of Same Boat Theatre Collective, and a member of the Pear Writers' Guild and the Dramatists' Guild. She earned an MFA in creative writing from Spalding University.

EXPOSURE
appeared in the
2019 Red Bull Theater Short New Play Festival:
The Evil Plays

CAST OF CHARACTERS

King. Male, 20s-40s. Recently usurped the throne.

Shepherd. Any gender, 50+. Has seen a lot. Doesn't suffer fools.

Setting: The mythic past. A hillside on a warm summer night.
Running Time: Ten minutes.

EXPOSURE

Sometime in the mythical past. A grassy hillside on a warm summer night. Enter KING, dressed in a hooded cloak and golden sandals. He holds a bundled, sleeping infant. He places the baby on the ground, gives it a look— contempt, with maybe just a hint of pity— and turns to exit.

SHEPHERD (O/S)

Hey!

KING jumps guiltily and moves to stand in front of infant as SHEPHERD enters.

Where is that gods-damned sign? Sheep must've eaten it again. Look— this is a baby-free zone. Hear me? No leaving babies on this hillside.

KING

Uh...

That's not mine.

Glances at baby.

SHEPHERD

My condolences. You still can't leave it here.

KING

No— I mean it was here when I got here.

SHEPHERD

I just saw you put it down and start skulking away.

KING

No you didn't.

SHEPHERD

I've been a shepherd all my life. My night vision's 20/20. I know what I saw.

KING takes out and offers a few gold coins.

KING

I said: no you didn't.

> ## SHEPHERD

Not worth it.

> ## KING

What isn't?

> ## SHEPHERD

Getting involved in your dirty work.

> ## KING

I'm not involving you; I'm ordering you to stand aside. You'll go home. I'll go home. *That* will die of exposure, and both of us will forget this ever happened. I don't see the problem.

> ## SHEPHERD

That's not how this works.

> ## KING

What do you mean?

> ## SHEPHERD

I mean that's not how this story goes. Look, you're some kind of royalty, aren't you?

> ## KING

Why do you say that?

> ## SHEPHERD

Because I know your type. The imperious tone, the hubris, the lack of appropriate footwear for a hillside littered with dung. Gold sandals— really?

> > *(beat)*

Very well.

> > *KING removes his hood to reveal a crown.*

> ## KING

I'm the new king. *Your* new king.

> > *KING waits for a reaction, but SHEPHERD remains unimpressed.*

> ## SHEPHERD

Thought so. And that's what, your stepchild? Illegitimate offspring of your wife and a god?

Beat.

KING

Nephew.

SHEPHERD

Ah. Then you're royally screwed.

KING

Why?

SHEPHERD

Nothing ever ends well for evil uncles.

KING

I'm not *evil*. Just dealing with a— uniquely difficult situation.

SHEPHERD

There was a prophecy, right?

(*pause*)

Well?

KING

Possibly.

SHEPHERD

That the kid there will grow up to kill you and/or take back your stolen kingdom. Something like that, right? Plus or minus a generation or two?

It wasn't—

Beat.

KING

There may have been a minor dispute over whether I'm the legitimate heir to the throne. A debate over a technicality. It happens all the time during political transitions.

SHEPHERD

Whatever you've got to tell yourself. Point is, you're leaving that baby here out of some misbegotten notion it'll solve your problems. You're only stabbing yourself in the foot.

                    KING

And why is that?

                  SHEPHERD

What exactly do you think is going to happen to that baby? Walk me through
this, your Majesty.

                    KING

It'll die.

                  SHEPHERD

Of?

                    KING

Of... you know. The elements.

                  SHEPHERD

It's a balmy summer night.

                    KING

Starvation, then.

                  SHEPHERD

How long do you think that'll take?

                    KING

I don't know, an hour? Two?

                  SHEPHERD

Guess again. That kid's gonna be wailing here all night long. How possible do
you think it is that someone— most likely a shepherd who's too soft-hearted for
their own good— is going to find him and feel obligated to raise him?

                    KING

I... suppose it's possible.

                  SHEPHERD

Twenty years down the road, that kid's gonna show up at your doorstep with a
dagger and some well-rehearsed insults. In the meantime, I have to take care
of another child— in all likelihood one with superhuman strength who eats
enough for ten, and who has a cartload of abandonment issues to sort through
before he's ready to go kill you. I like quietude. I like lambs. They're cute and
they don't talk back. I'm gods-damned tired of raising people's enchanted
babies.

> **KING**

I'm not asking you to raise it.

> **SHEPHERD**

But now I know he's there.

> **KING**

Just ignore it.

> **SHEPHERD**

And listen to the Child of Destiny slowly crying himself to death on my hillside while my sheep graze twenty feet away? Do you think I want bring the gods' wrath on me?

> **KING**

Give it an hour. Maybe an animal will come along.

> **SHEPHERD**

I've yet to see a sheep go after a baby.

> **KING**

I mean a carnivore. A wolf, or something.

> **SHEPHERD**

What kind of shepherd would I be if I let wolves prowl around here? Besides, there's no guarantee the wolf would eat it. If it's a she-wolf, she's just as likely to suckle it. More kids get raised by wolves than you'd imagine. And then you've got to deal with a guy who not only wants you dead, but who's probably developed a taste for raw flesh.

> **KING**

Okay, how about a— a vulture? Vultures can't suckle children. They don't have teats.

> *(beat)*

Do they?

> **SHEPHERD**

Thanks for that image. I told you: this is *your* dirty work. Deal with it yourself. Take that baby somewhere else. Or, here's an unorthodox and brilliant idea: *just kill him.*

> **KING**

I— no.

SHEPHERD

Why not? It's the obvious solution. And don't do something stupid like lock him in a tower or throw him in the river— that *doesn't work*. If it were me, I'd cut off his head and keep it with me for a couple of weeks for good measure. You never know.

KING

Fine. You do it, then.

SHEPHERD

This is between you and the Fates.

KING

I *command* you to do it.

SHEPHERD

And I'm telling you I won't.

KING

I could have you put to death.

SHEPHERD

That wouldn't solve your problems.

KING

It'll solve one of them— a cheeky shepherd.

SHEPHERD

Oh, gods, now look what you've done.

KING

What? What have I done?

SHEPHERD

We've slipped into stichomythia.

KING

What the hell is stichomythia?

SHEPHERD

An exchange of alternating one-liners.

KING

We're just having an argument.

SHEPHERD

One that conforms to a predictable pattern.

KING

You're making that up to change the subject.

SHEPHERD

It's not my fault you're a walking trope.

KING

Stop responding with a single line!

SHEPHERD

Stop setting me up with one!

KING

How do we get out of this?

SHEPHERD

Just shut up for a second.

They pause. Silence.

I think we're good.

KING
(taking out coins again)

Look, how much do you want? I'll give you all of this, and throw in the gold sandals.

SHEPHERD

I told you— not worth it.

KING

You can buy a dozen more hillsides. More sheep than you can count.

SHEPHERD

I'm good on sheep. I'm not killing that baby for you. Why won't you do it yourself?

KING

Because I...

SHEPHERD

What's the problem? You're ruthless enough to usurp a throne but not to kill a baby?

KING

It's beneath me. I don't want blood on these regal hands.

SHEPHERD

Oh, please. I bet you killed his parents and stuck their heads on pikes.

KING

That was— different.

SHEPHERD

If you can't even subdue your guilty conscience, you have no business ruling a city.

KING

My conscience isn't guilty! I'm doing what I have to.

SHEPHERD

In a highly roundabout way.

KING

It's just... it would be crude. Butchering it like an animal.

SHEPHERD

Hell of a lot more humane than leaving him to slowly starve.

KING

But it's just not... I don't know. Poetic.

SHEPHERD

Poetic? Coming from the guy who didn't know what stichomythia was? This is a load of manure, your Majesty. Tell me the truth.

KING

I— I— see myself in him!

SHEPHERD

Now we're getting somewhere.

KING

Damn it. I see myself in that scrunched-up, ugly little face. I mean— not that he *looks* like me; he's got more of my brother's profile. But he reminds me of myself. When I was a baby—

SHEPHERD

Something tells me we're heading into a long monologue capped by a moment of self-discovery.

KING

Do you want to hear this or not?

SHEPHERD sits down.

SHEPHERD

Ready. Go on.

KING

When I was a baby, my parents left me on a hillside to die. And yes, I was rescued. *Not* by a shepherd.

(beat)

It was a wood nymph. I grew up thinking I was a nobody, thrown away, someone's unwanted bastard, destined to spend my worthless life as a farmer or a fisherman or a shepherd. No offense. As it turns out, I *was* illegitimate, but I was the bastard of a *king*, one who left me on that hillside so his queen wouldn't find me. By the time I learned the truth, my philandering father was already dead, but I had a lazy, inattentive younger half-brother on the throne. It was mine for the taking. *What.* I saw an opportunity and I seized it. Don't tell me you wouldn't have done the same thing. I taught myself how to fight, I gathered an army, and I ousted him. And yes, there may have been some pikes and dismemberment involved; it happens. Everything was going swimmingly until the royal prophetess showed me that *damned baby* hidden away in the palace, my ugly little newborn nephew— half-nephew, really— and said, "If this child lives, he will rule your kingdom." That was it. There wasn't even any ambiguity to it, like there usually is in these things. You know, "Beware of the cross-eyed turtle on the mountain at twilight." No. No weirdness here. It was impossible to misread, like the old crone dumbed it down just for me. And how do you think I felt? After all I went through— all I did to find my confidence and inner strength and overcome my deep-seated feelings of inferiority— now I find out that *destiny itself* might be working against me? Good gods! What else can I do but get rid of the threat? What would *you* do? Why do you keep judging me? Am I really the villain here— just because I'm putting my own needs before everyone else's, sacrificing the life of an innocent baby, and quite possibly defying the gods? Because seriously, if that's your definition of *evil,* then I... I...

KING (CONT'D)

Well, I suppose if... Oh. Shit.

Pause.

KING sits down slowly as SHEPHERD stands.

SHEPHERD

For what it's worth, your Majesty, I'm not completely convinced you *have* to be the villain.

KING

What?

SHEPHERD

You might— just might— be able to turn things around and become a flawed hero. If you're willing to stomach a major plot twist.

KING

I'm listening.

SHEPHERD

You could take the kid home. Raise him yourself.

KING

Raise him? Like... an actual baby?

SHEPHERD

Raise him as your heir, and then, when the time comes, pass the kingdom to him. That way the prophecy's fulfilled, but he doesn't have to kill you. Win-win.

KING

I— I can't. I don't know how to be a father. I never had one.

SHEPHERD

Do your best. If you need advice from time to time, I'll be here.

KING

How am I supposed to feed it?

SHEPHERD

I'd be happy to give you a discount on sheep's milk.

> *KING stands. He stares at baby. At last, gingerly and awkwardly, he picks him up. The baby wakes and starts crying. King soothes him back to sleep.*

KING

It's— *he's*— not quite as ugly as I thought.

SHEPHERD

See? Bonding already. Although...

KING

What?

SHEPHERD

It'd be pretty awkward if he ever finds out you murdered and mutilated his real parents.

KING

I won't tell him. I'll pass him off as my own son.

SHEPHERD

It's a shame someone else knows the truth. If only there were a way to make that person hold their tongue.

KING

Are you blackmailing me?

SHEPHERD

I saw an opportunity and I seized it.

KING

Fine, what do you want?

> *SHEPHERD points to KING's golden sandals. King takes them off and hands them over grudgingly.*

SHEPHERD

Best of luck to you both! Ooh— watch out for the dung.

> *KING, now barefoot, exits with baby.*

> *End of play.*

Nineteen Twenty-Six

by

David Lerner Schwartz
& Sofya Levitsky-Weitz

DAVID LERNER SCHWARTZ

David Lerner Schwartz teaches writing and literature at the University of Cincinnati, where he is a doctoral student. His work has been published in *New Ohio Review, Los Angeles Review, Witness, SmokeLong Quarterly, Literary Hub, New York* magazine, *The Rumpus,* and more. His writing has been supported by grants and fellowships from UC's Department of English and Niehoff Center for Film & Media Studies, Bread Loaf Writers' Conference, and the Bennington Writing Seminars, from which he holds an MFA. He served as the 38th writer in residence at St. Albans and works as the fiction editor of *Four Way Review.* davidlernerschwartz.com

SOFYA LEVITSKY-WEITZ

Sofya Levitsky-Weitz lives in Brooklyn and Los Angeles. She's written for Hulu's *The Dropout*, FX's *The Bear*, and *Gaslit* for Starz. Her play *this party sucks* will be produced by Mark Gordon Pictures next year and was on the 2019 Kilroy's List. Other plays include *Cannabis Passover* (PWC PlayLabs, 2020-2021 finalist for the O'Neill Playwrights' Conference), *be mean to me* (semi-finalist for Premiere Stages at Keane), *Gehinnom* (semi-finalist for O'Neill Playwrights' Conference, Playwrights' Realm, and Princess Grace Award), and *Intuitive Men* (UCF Pegasus Playlab). She was a 2018-2019 Jerome Fellow and is a current Core Writer at the Playwrights' Center in Minneapolis. Residencies with the MacDowell Colony, Barn Arts, and TOFTE. She served as the script consultant for Michael Showalter for Fox Searchlight's *The Eyes of Tammy Faye* and received the 2020-2021 New Musical Commission for Penn State. She got her MFA in Writing for the Screen & Stage from Northwestern University, where she serves on the advisory board, and is a member of EST/Youngblood. www.sofyalevitskyweitz.com

NINETEEN TWENTY-SIX
appeared in the
2019 Red Bull Theater Short New Play Festival:
The Evil Plays

CAST OF CHARACTERS

Edie. A casino dealer, badass.

Azazel. A false angel.

Setting: A casino in the desert. Maybe it's a mirage.
Time: Right now but also back then.
Running Time: Approximately fifteen minutes.

A NOTE FROM THE AUTHORS

Why, in the Bible, does Lot's wife become a pillar of salt? The book doesn't give us her name, only her demise: fleeing Sodom's destruction by God, she looks once more toward her city against instruction. Our play follows her, a woman we call Edie, a casino dealer. We wanted to know what might make someone turn back knowing full well the cost.

This project arose from a longing to understand the backstories and interiors of female characters in the Bible, inner lives that are mostly absent. Reverend Lindsay Hardin Freeman found that the 93 women who speak in the text— only 49 of whom are named— contribute to 1.1% of its total words.

These women are instead often tools for exploring the complexities of male protagonists, or foils to highlight lessons that live on in male reigns. We have much to learn in revealing the absent female perspectives of one of the most widely read and translated texts in the world. Though some believe the Bible includes retellings of the past, others believe it's a code to teach us who we are. By re-embodying myth with newfound history and agency, could we begin to re-embody ourselves as well?

Our interest goes beyond theme. We were hungry for grittiness, messiness, the *realness* that transcends allegory. Lot's wife is a singular person made into archetype. By writing *Nineteen*, we were hoping to look at the minutiae that makes one woman who she is and how her experiences might add up to that most certain decision. We sought to reinhabit a reference.

And we also just wrote, and this is what came out.

In 2019, we saw Lot's wife come to life. She swears. She sprints. And she looks right back at us, as us.

Directed by Vivienne Benesch, Producing Artistic Director at Playmakers Repertory Company.

NINETEEN TWENTY-SIX

*There's a projection of a casino onstage. The sign
says HOUSE OF MAMMON but the last "o" isn't lit.
We are somewhere in the desert. This is some sort of
oasis.*

*From offstage, recorded, we hear, like through a
paging system, or microphone, a bored male voice:*

*"Flee for your life. Do not look back, and do not stop
anywhere on the Plain. Flee to the mountains, or you
will be swept away."*

*EDIE comes out. She's in her late 30s, early 40s.
She looks great. She's in a fur coat, because, come
on, she's in a fucking fur coat.*

*She takes out a cigarette. She sets it on the ground,
gently.*

*She starts doing stretches, arm past her shoulder,
other arm. Arms above her head, she bends over.
We see she has a gun tucked into her skirt.*

She sees the cigarette on the ground.

*She picks it up again. She looks at it. She doesn't
light it.*

She puts it in her mouth for a moment. Takes it out.

EDIE

This is me, running.

*The projection changes and suddenly House of
Mammon is farther away.*

You don't want to see that, though.
That'll just look—
I'll be all breathless and
my nose will probably be runny
and I'll get a side cramp
because I don't drink enough water.
At some point, the endorphins will kick in,
that fight-or-flight stuff, like this is it.
This is all I have right now, and I'll run

EDIE (CONT'D)
really fast— I trained my daughters to sprint—
and maybe I'll feel so overwhelmed that I
cry, or I sing along to my favorite pop song; I'll
throw my fist to the beat,
but you don't want to see that either.

> *AZAZEL walks onstage, faces front. He is dressed in suspenders and a button-down, like he runs a speakeasy.*

I bought the gun because I needed it.
...That's a lie—
I lie a lot.

People say that, *I needed it.*
"I feared for my life."
"I was scared."

None of that is true.
It doesn't matter what we need,
although, I figured it would come in handy.

Which is sort of similar— you know,
I've had this thought since I was little.
It's always ringing so true in my brain:

I am evil and I invite evil.

I've known every decision I make is in service of it.
And so buying the gun,
it just felt natural.

> *EDIE looks at AZAZEL, who very specifically cleans, loads, and cocks an invisible gun.*

AZAZEL
We've got Ruger 10/22 rifles,
a Bushmaster Carbon 15 M4 Carbine,
Henry Arms AR-7,
glocks of all kinds,
Sig Sauer P226,
Taurus Judge,

>   AZAZEL (CONT'D)
Mossberg 590 Mariner,
I mean really take your pick.
Do you want me to pick for you?

>   *She looks at us.*

>   EDIE
I'm the type of person who thought I'd stay alone forever.
I liked my solitude—
I liked my life.
I've never had any choice in any person who ever decided to love me.
They just did,
and suddenly— there were little black hairs in my basin,
canvas pants rumpled up next to my bed,
meat cooking on the grill,
always meat.

>   *(to Azazel)*
A Rough Rider.
Do you have that?

>   AZAZEL
We have—
that.

>   *AZAZEL goes to get it. EDIE stretches, pulls her hair*
>   *up into a ponytail.*

>   EDIE
Hence the gun.

>   *EDIE holds the cigarette again, considers lighting it.*

When Lot would rock me in bed, sometimes he would cry into my hair.
Sometimes when I would come,
he'd look at me like: what *happens to you* in that moment?
That stupefying minute—
that place between blame and mystery.
They just won't ever know,
and so, you know,

>   *She gestures her hands to the world.*

there's this.

AZAZEL returns, hands her the gun.

AZAZEL
Here. Thank you, miss—

EDIE
No, really, I appreciate—

She digs in her bag for money.

AZAZEL
(stopping her)
Wait. How about something different?

The sounds of the casino become sharper.

What if we play?
If I win, you can pay me.
If you win, you get it for free.
How's that?

EDIE
(laughing, interested)
Okay, okay.

EDIE and AZAZEL play a game of blackjack as Edie speaks.

Let me back up.
Lot is my husband. He's the one you've heard about.
I'm the possessive.
They can't even agree on my name.

We've been married nearly twenty years.

I met him when I was dealing at the casino. You know the one—
it has the lights, the sign. The letter's missing.
It's like a joke at this point, and no one feels a need to change it.
Because, I guess, tradition.

EDIE has 19. We see this.

We've all played before.
Highest hand up to 21 and score.
I think you need to be a little off to even
attempt to try; I mean,

                    EDIE (CONT'D)
ties go to the dealer,
the house always wins, in the end, turns out.
That's how this stuff works.
Do a Monte Carlo simulation.
It's all loaded the wrong way.

But there is a thrill to me, a teetering on the edge—
I am *always* teetering on some edge. Risk.
I was born on a mountain.
I remember staring off toward the stars.
I sought what was level.
So here I am, the Plain.

                    AZAZEL
Stay.

                    EDIE
Evil is liking most when the odds are against you.

                    EDIE pulls a 7.

Shit, twenty-six.
Shit, I had nineteen, then twenty-six.

                    AZAZEL
So, pay.

                    EDIE pays.

Double.

                    *EDIE rifles through her bag for more money, slowing
                    as finds less and less.*

                    EDIE
But what about licking?
What about the tongue?

                    *The projection changes again, and the casino is even
                    farther away.*

I'm running because all of this will soon be destroyed.
No, not by me.
Like I have that kind of power.

EDIE (CONT'D)

Like I don't.
My chicken-shit husband took off at the first sign of destruction—
I'm sorry, that was ungenerous of me:
my husband isn't chicken-shit,
he's just deeply cowardly.

In the end
he doesn't think evil is a thing that can be loved,
so he refuses to think that I could be it, in a way.
There's no grey with men, because it's all just survival:
he took our girls, told me to grab our things.
I was busy searching for the gun.
He always needed to be first.
He left.

> *AZAZEL walks to a stage with a microphone and a bugle.*
>
> *He is performing some sort of stand-up set. EDIE goes over and sits in his audience.*

EDIE

For our twentieth anniversary, we went out—
I spiked my tea at the dark table with a little bottle of absinthe
I carry around in my underwear.
The comic was doing a bit—
"The Top 10 Reasons a Gun Is Better Than a Girl."

AZAZEL

10. You can trade an old .44 for a new .22
9. You can keep one gun at home and have another for when you're on the road
8. If you admire a friend's gun and tell him so, he will probably let you try it out a few times
7. Your primary gun doesn't mind if you keep another gun for a backup
6. Your gun will stay with you even if you run out of ammo
5. A gun doesn't take up a lot of closet space
4. A gun functions normally every day of the month
3. A gun doesn't ask, "Does this new scope make me look fat?"
2. A gun doesn't mind if you go to sleep right after you use it
And the number one reason a gun is better than a woman:

EDIE (CONT'D)

1. You can buy a silencer for a gun!

> *Another recording, this time of bored male laughter.*
> *A guffaw.*

> *EDIE laughs along. She's playing, participating, and*
> *makes this clear.*

EDIE

I know I should tell you about last night.

> *EDIE puts on an apron.*

Last night,
I made dinner, though I didn't try very hard.
We warmed it up, and everything was the same color.
I only cook in beige.
I once told my mother that, and now I'm cursed.
My daughters complained of course. They whispered to each other—
they're always whispering—
they don't make eye contact.
Lot watched the window screens, chewed and chewed.
It's not good to him unless it's all meat.

And then—
last night, we were visited by angels.
This happens sometimes.

> *AZAZEL walks into EDIE's home. She's cleaning up*
> *dinner. She points the gun at him.*

Get the hell out of my house!

AZAZEL

You and your family need to leave.
Tomorrow—

> *(gestures)*

this will all be gone.

EDIE
> *(to audience)*

I only bought the gun to protect myself,
for if I was truly in danger,
which is why when I pulled the trigger

EDIE (CONT'D)
the angel didn't even flinch.

> *AZAZEL sets up a table for EDIE. It's the whole thing: the card table, the chips. She drops the fur coat and the apron, and she's in a blazer. This is a legit dealer. She's going to do the damn thing.*

> *She deals a whole game almost silently. She points to each person to whom she's dealing, but we can't see them. Maybe someone declines, another one takes a hit. Someone gets out.*

(flipping cards)
You had nineteen, then twenty-six.

(looking up)
Our daughters followed close behind Lot.
One was crying out for her husband,
the other one looking only ahead,
always straight ahead, like I taught her.
One day, she will forget what I look like.

And so then there's me, at the back. With the gun.
Running. Still running.

I did not have a name they could call—
and so they didn't.

> *EDIE stands as the casino is cleared. The projection changes another time: it is now the Plain. It is nothingness, emptiness. Just limestone and beige bullshit. The fucking desert.*

> *She holds the cigarette again.*

> *She slowly becomes a pillar of salt.*

Do you want the truth?
I *am* the salt.
When I fired at the angel,
I wanted something to happen.

> *AZAZEL stands behind EDIE. Maybe a video of Edie's face is projected behind Azazel.*

AZAZEL

Flee for your life. Do not look back,
and do not stop anywhere on the Plain.
Flee to the mountains, or you will be
swept away.

EDIE

So I was running,
am, running.
Always: running.

Until I stopped,
and I turned,
to gaze upon my city.

Blackout.

End of play.

The Devil of History

by

Matthew Wells

MATTHEW WELLS

Matthew Wells is a Thailand-based playwright and poet whose productions include *Schrödinger's Girlfriend* (EST Sloan Grant; Magic Theatre, San Francisco; Act II Playhouse, Ambler PA); *Oscar and Adonis* (2000 Tennessee Williams Literary Festival One-Act Play Award); *Scarlet Woman* (2011 Frigid Festival, NYC; Edmonton Fringe; Winnipeg Fringe; Gremlin Theatre, St. Paul); *Beautiful Day* (finalist, 2013 Lark Playwrights Week; Actors Theatre of Charlotte's 2016 nuVoices Festival); *Countrie Matters* (2015 Great Plains Theatre Conference; 2020 Fall Festival, Arizona Theatre Matters); *Romeo and Rosaline* (2015 Red Bull Theater Short Play Festival); *Elvis at Auschwitz* (Nylon Fusion); *Barabbas* (semi-finalist, 2017 National Playwrights Conference); and *Falstaff In Love (*Finalist, 2018 Shakespeare's New Contemporaries). He posts a daily rhymed couplet on the Facebook page The Daily Couplet, and he is the author of five unfinished novels and a work-in-progress entitled "100 Things I'll Never Have The Time To Write."

THE DEVIL OF HISTORY
appeared in the
2019 Red Bull Theater Short New Play Festival:
The Evil Plays

CAST OF CHARACTERS

Iago. (M) Ageless. Articulate. Reasonable. And a bit of a condescending prick. Not an ounce of doubt in his body.

Setting: A courtroom. The final moments of Iago's trial for murder.

Running Time: Approximately ten minutes.

A NOTE FROM THE AUTHOR

Writing *The Devil of History* gave me an opportunity to address three things—Iago's "motiveless malignity," as Coleridge called it; the idea that, when human beings do evil, they are almost always evicted from the human race and called inhuman monsters; and the common belief that an omnipotent deity is actually subject to morality, which would make the morality omnipotent and not the god. It also gave me a chance to stretch my blank verse muscles, and allow a clever man on the point of death not just to make his case before the world, but to do it in such a way that it haunts their dreams. This is a play in which "I am not a monster; I am one of you," becomes the wolf's taunt to the sheep: "You too can be a wolf; and that is why you're executing me."

THE DEVIL OF HISTORY

IAGO, center stage.

He is loving every minute of this.

IAGO

You ask me why I plotted 'gainst the Moor,
As if some truth from my deceiving lips
Can be the pillow for your sleepless nights,
As if an answer cancels out a question
And saves the world from death or worse. The world.
The world's disturbed by what is out of place
And reasons not the need to know the reason
Behind a man's actions, so it can map
Him city, street and house, within the mobbed
Commonwealth of the soul, showing the road
From where a man like you, who lives his life
Far from the verge, might stray into the wild
And find himself upon the cliff, like me,
As far as possible from common ground,
Yet still penned in a comprehended place.
So do your questions use cartography
To prove that someone who is off the map
Is just a citizen who turned traitor,
And not some orphan from that nameless space
Whose only legend is, "Here there be dragons."

Myself, I don't believe that Reason can
Explain the awful things man does to man.
And as for Faith, while it might hush your doubts,
There is a reason why the faithful are
Always compared to sheep. Frightened of silence
More than they are of death, the wild devout
Petition heaven just to make some noise—
Their prayers, as thick as slander from a fraud,
Like darting tongues inside the ear of God—
A god for those with nothing left to lose,
The just Divinity of slaves and women
And all who thirst for justice in the next world
Because it is as distant and unreachable

IAGO (CONT'D)

As God in this one. Pray all you want, but
My crimes beggar the charity of any
Forgiving God, just as they bankrupt all
Your worthy mitigations of my wrongs.
You clip me thus and so, cutting your cloth
Of metaphrastic worsted till it fits
The height of my transgressions— yet there will
Always be something that sticks out, some length
Of wrist or leg that never will be covered
By your sewing— some flash of human flesh
Peeping behind my monster suit— and then
All that you've fashioned to me will unravel.

You say that weakness is the devil's feast—
He dines with those who keep a chair for him,
Then walks away and leaves them with the reckoning
Because they were not strong enough to say
No to an evil appetite. I say
There is a strength in sin that earns respect,
For why else would the virtuous attempt
To shrink evil down to belittled size?
"Pure evil's much too dangerous to be
Potential in us all— it must be rare;
It must be owed to some defect of nature,
Some flaw i' the diamond of the human soul,
And not the gem itself. It is the seed,
The evil poisoned seed that blossoms blood,
And not the general crop, and not the garden."

So would you blame the poison seed in me,
If you could find a ripe one in my past—
Accuse my father (if I even had one)
Of some abuse that's physical or mental;
Point to my mother and the way she did
Or did not give me love; chart Venice streets
Until you find one that corrupted me;
Say that when I say hate, I speak of love,
Or that I was consumed with jealousy,

IAGO (CONT'D)

Or thought the world was wrong and I was right
(As if self-righteousness forgives a wrong)—
Or hated black because it was not white.
Or like the wise, removed philosopher,
Proclaim that in a reasonable world
No man does wrong knowing that he does wrong;
He does wrong out of ignorance or madness—
Therefore I must be ignorant or mad.

Say what you will. Myself,
I say awareness is immediate,
And Time pearls over the offending itch
Of conscience till it gleams with ignorance.
And I know how unthinkable that is
For you to fathom. All depths have a bottom,
So you sound for a cause; it is the cause
Iago hides that makes Iago whole.
It can be anything from sin to sneer
To proof undoubted of insanity—
Anything to smooth me out small and tidy
Because you cannot bring yourselves to say
That what I did, I did because I did.
Is not evil no more than that— the voice
Of one who cries, "I can, therefore I will?"
A shallow bottom for your deep distress.
To think that evil's only ankle deep
And not some dark unfathomable beast—
No wonder you can't sleep. I wouldn't either
If I were you. But I am not. I doze
Like a well-suckled baby in the arms
Of his attentive mother, and that slumber
Will never be disturbed by thoughts of why
This soul may shine while that soul casts a shadow.
And never once be troubled by the fear
Of retribution from a God who says
All evil must be punished.

                    Spare me that,
Or kill me now, for I do not believe

IAGO (CONT'D)

That God believes in recompense for evil.
My soul has simply learned to sing a note
That yours objects to— though you all have that
Low note within your range— and could hit it,
Hit it as effortlessly as I do—
Without a thought. Without even a thought.
We tune the voices of our souls to sing
What pleases us; and there are just as many
Pleasures as there are people in this life.
Mine is not yours; yours never will be mine.
If that is evil, why then, God's at fault.

Oh yes. You heard me right. God is at fault.
You say to me that God will strike me down
For daring to insult Him. Here I stand.
You say to me that God will punish me.
I say to you, "Then why did He not stop me?"
You say to me that God believes in justice.
I say to you that God believes in sin,
Or else He would not punish it. I say
To you that God, who made the sun
And moon to battle for each day's dominion—
Who made the night a hornet's nest of fear
To buzz and sting the bosom of the day
And fill her heart with poison— that same God,
That same divine beneficent Creator,
Created evil. It is not that God
Allows bad things to happen, or permits
Disasters as a test against man's faith
In His great goodness. No— the truth is clear
And animates this world, and it is this:
This world of catastrophic imperfections
Is God's unfathomable perfect plan.
And if man's eyes were free from self-deception,
They would perceive that this all-good immortal
Vanishes with one touch of mortal logic.

One. God cannot be God if He is not
All-powerful. Two. If evil exists,

IAGO (CONT'D)

It cannot be more powerful than God.
Three. If good exists, then the same holds true:
It cannot be more powerful than God.
Therefore, God must be greater than both good
And evil, or He is not God. Therefore,
In this omnipotence which we call God
And look to as the fountain of all goodness,
There is no goodness. He looks down on it.
If He is truly God, then He has no
More morality than a piece of rope,
Which can be thrown to save a falling life
Or twisted into nooses to kill others.
God cannot be God if He looks up to
Goodness as something greater than Himself.
If He is God, then He's above it all.
And, like all those on earth who are above
It all, He looks down on disasters quite
Dispassionately, like a king looks down
On servant girls who die while giving birth.
And that is how God looks upon mankind:
He'll watch us die, playing the game He made—
Just like He made the heavens cup the earth;
Just like He made our minds to question Him;
Just like He made both good and evil, and
Iago.

If you still ask me why, then you are deaf.
All I can say is that you will go hungry
When your fat Why dines on my thin Because.
I was not born to reason like the Dane
Or point to friendly stars for latitude—
If you would chart my passage, then the tides
That lift all barks alike are what this dog
Obeyed in's office. Go, resolve my life,
And even though years are divisible
By days, and days by cause and influence,
You will not ever build a bridge between
My baby picture and the men I killed.
We are what others do not ever know

IAGO (CONT'D)

And will not ever miss. The best of us
Keep secrets that a saint would not forgive,
And know that God is like a master craftsman
Who loves his handiwork and tries it well,
Like one who tempers steel. And what God says
Is what the blacksmith says when he anneals
His favorite foils: "After this test, you fail."
So do you test me, and would see me break,
The elements within me catalogued
In due proportion, with the hopeful cry:
"After this answer, you will be explained."
But I will never be, not as long as
Virtue has doubts and Vice is always certain,
Goodness is gullible, Sin taste like wine,
And Ignorance is absolute for blood.
As all of you are absolute for mine—

For in your hearts, you know that this is true:
I did what you were too afraid to do.

> *IAGO smiles. It is not a humorous smile, but it sure is an attractive one.*
>
> *Slow fade.*
>
> *Blackout.*
>
> *End of play.*

Outside Time, Without Extension

by

Ben Beckley

BEN BECKLEY

Ben Beckley made his Broadway debut in *What The Constitution Means To Me*. He has premiered work by Tony-winners Itamar Moses and Christopher Durang, and OBIE-winners Kate Benson and Adam Rapp. Additional acting credits include the first national tours of *Peter and the Starcatcher* and *Small Mouth Sounds*, performances at Atlantic Theater Company, Denver Center, Center Theatre Group, Long Wharf, ACT, and Clubbed Thumb, as well as *Inventing Anna* (Netflix) and *Hair Wolf* (Sundance Short Film Jury Award).

As an actor and contributing writer, he's co-created six original projects with The Assembly, all dir. Jess Chayes, including the NY Times Critics' Pick *HOME/SICK*, which explores political radicalism in the late '60s, and the dystopian musical *In Corpo*.

Other writing credits include *Anno Dominorum* (F*It Club) and *Latter Days* (Dutch Kills/Ars Nova), as well as two time-bending augmented reality projects with designer/theatermaker Asa Wember: *KlaxAlterian Sequester* (www.klaxalteria.com) and *Junction*.

www.benbeckley.com

OUTSIDE TIME, WITHOUT EXTENSION
appeared in the
2020 Red Bull Theater Short New Play Festival:
Private Lives

CAST OF CHARACTERS

David. Male-identifying, any race, the age that he is now; eager to believe things aren't as bleak as they seem.

Neoptolemus. Female-identifying, any race, the age that she is now; perennially bright.

Setting: Two chairs (optional).
Running Time: Ten minutes (100 years).

A slash (/), indicating an overlap, cues the other character to start speaking. Brackets ([]) indicates words thought, but not spoken.

A NOTE FROM THE AUTHOR

Every play is, I suppose, a sort of balancing act between "craft" and "reality."

Typically, the playwright offers us enough information that we know what's going on and enough mystery that we're excited to find out what happens next, the actors speak clearly and loudly enough that we can understand every word, and a minute of stage time translates to a minute of the characters' lived experience. And conventions like these are useful, because they make it easier for us to understand the play— and, through the play, the world.

But if we start to experiment with different conventions, we end up with a different kind of play, that points to a different understanding of the world. Adjusting the craft alters our sense of reality. In *Outside Time, Without Extension*, for example, a minute of stage time translates to ten years of the characters' lived experience.

And that atypical convention pulls the audience, I hope, in two very different directions. On the one hand, because it's a convention that calls attention to itself, it may remind us how plays don't just reflect but refract human experience. And on the other hand, it may make us think more about our own lived experience: fraught, beautiful, and brief. Weirdly, in making us more aware of how reality is represented in the play, it brings us closer to that reality.

Art is artificial. And art is life.

(Or, more accurately, it can be tough to tell the difference.)

And if you're someone who loves reading (or writing) books and watching (or making) plays, you may find, pretty soon, that it becomes impossible to untangle them from your own experiences, that what might have begun as a search for a way to process the world has (more or less) become the world.

A NOTE FROM THE AUTHOR (cont'd)

Anyway, this is a play about all those things. And loneliness and anxiety and love. And about two people who (like my wife and I) find meaning, and sometimes comfort, in literature, and in each other.

And, like life, it's pretty short.

Outside Time, Without Extension premiered at Red Bull Theater's Short New Play Festival in July 2020. The cast (William Jackson Harper as David and Ali Ahn as Sarah) was directed by Vivienne Benesch.

A workshop production, dir. Virginia Ogden, was performed at Northern Stage in January 2020. That cast featured Holden Harris as David and Lexi Warden as Sarah.

OUTSIDE TIME, WITHOUT EXTENSION

DAVID turns to the audience.

DAVID

Thank you for coming.

He rings a bell and starts a stopwatch.

This is a ten-minute play.

If each minute of this play represents one decade, and I'm born at the sound of the bell, then by the end of this sentence, I'm already walking and talking.

I'm David.

I'm alone right now. Sarah hasn't been born yet.

Alone except my parents and the staff at Jackson Memorial.

SARAH rings a bell and starts a stopwatch.

SARAH

Hi, I'm Sarah.

DAVID

And now also our neighbors, the Sunbys. They brought over a pie when my folks brought me home from the hospital. That was three years ago. I'm already three years old.

And now I'm four.

When time moves so fast, it's hard to keep up.

SARAH

I'm three years younger. David and I don't know each other, which is why we're not looking at each other now.

DAVID

All alone except my parents, the Sunbys, and Matt, who's my best friend at school. (I'm five.)

DAVID rings a bell.

And that's my sister Alex.

But none of those people exist in this play. Not in the same way that we do.

SARAH

The two of us won't meet for another eighty seconds. Or thirteen years.

DAVID

Showing you everyone would get complicated. I mean, where would it end?

SARAH

Better to keep it simple.
I'm seven years old, and I'm reading *Charlotte's Web.*

SARAH rings a bell.

(re: the bell)
That's Patrick, my little brother. I read to him, but there's not much he understands.

DAVID

Matt is my best friend. And so is Debbie. And sometimes Emmett.
Sarah and I live 678 miles apart. We still haven't met.

SARAH

I grow up outside Chicago and he's from Southern Virginia.

DAVID

Some kid stole my backpack. Debbie's a bitch. Matt stopped talking to me.
Middle school's a nightmare.

SARAH

I'm reading Harry Potter. I like the Sorting Hat.

DAVID

I can't wait til it's over.
It's over.

SARAH

Nice to know there's a place for you.

DAVID

High school is weird. I'm reading *The Stranger.*

SARAH

I finished *The Goblet of Fire.*

DAVID

I'm reading *No Exit*.
My parents have something to tell me. They're splitting up.

SARAH

Deathly Hallows. Eh. She could use an editor.

DAVID

Brave New World.
Emmett kills himself.

SARAH

Borges. Garcia Marquez. The world feels bigger than it was before.

DAVID

Endgame. Dorian Gray.
I write my first story, about a kid who's got a sense that time is moving faster than he can comprehend and what even *is* reality if not perspective but then what does anyone understand about the universe really except that it's bearing down upon us.

SARAH

Allende. Morrison.

DAVID

And then he has a breakdown.

SARAH

Kafka. Keats. Yeats. Woolf. Joyce.

DAVID

And then I have a breakdown.

SARAH

Ulysses. To The Lighthouse.

DAVID

I spend the next ten days in the hospital. I take a year off from college.

SARAH

And I'm writing too. I'm exploring the narrative strategies authors use to integrate fiction and nonfiction.
Clark Kent works in Delaware, across the bay from Gotham. Hogwarts and Brigadoon are in the Scottish Highlands. Roy Cohn is an actual person but the

SARAH (CONT'D)

Angel of History is not. James Joyce has a double vision of the everyday Dublin he knows and the ancient Greek epic he's only read. And they're both equally real to him.

And I think that's inevitable— that double vision. Because an author can't help but draw on both her own, lived experience and on narrative's inherent artificiality. Because when you tell a story, you're saying something about who you are and also what a story is.

You may think coming from an eighth-grader these observations sound a little implausible, but by now I'm a sophomore in college.

Oh, and that's where we meet.

> *They look at each other for the first time.*
>
> *Time slows down.*
> *(For them, if not their stopwatches.)*

Hey.

DAVID

Hm.

SARAH

Can I...?

DAVID

Sorry yeah, have a seat if you—
I was just, um, reading.

> *It's OK if the actor playing Sarah is already sitting. It's OK if the actor playing David doesn't have a book.*

SARAH

I'm Sarah.

DAVID

Cool.

SARAH

And what's your...?

DAVID

Oh. David.

                    SARAH

Nice to meet you, David.

                    DAVID

Absolutely.
I mean— you too.

                    Maybe one of them smiles.

Man... After midterms, I'm always... [out of it.]

                    SARAH

No, same.

                    DAVID

Yeah.

                    SARAH

I've heard that's great.

                    DAVID

?

                    SARAH
             (re: David's copy of Don Quixote*)*

The book. That class.

                    DAVID

Have you taken it?

                    She hasn't.

                    SARAH

You like it?

                    DAVID

It's... yeah, pretty... [great].
It's reframed everything. For me.
Or reminded me that everything *is* a frame, you know what I...?

                    She doesn't.

Well, because his whole point— Cervantes— is smashing together old medieval
fantasies and real stuff happening now, in Spain, during the Inquisition. And
you'd think the knights and giants would be the crazy stuff, right— they're
definitely crazy-making for Quixote— but in fact the actual, supposedly rational

DAVID (CONT'D)

world is full of, you know, book burnings, auto de fe, peasants pooping themselves— Sorry, don't mean to—

She's not offended.

But my point is once you start to see the thing from two different sides, that changes you, not just how you read this, but how you read everything, anything, maybe the way you *live*, even.

SARAH

A double vision. The author's and the character's.

DAVID

Yeah.

Or even, like, life and the meaning of life: experience and interpretation.

SARAH

Though in Cervantes' case the character is authoring his own experience and the writer's skeptical of the definitive interpretive authority of authorship.

DAVID

Huh, sure— competing prisms.

SARAH

Like two mirrors facing each other.

DAVID

Yeah. They amplify the image. Reproduce it.

They both ding their bells.

SARAH

And maybe that double image is what makes you aware that what you're looking at *is* an image.

DAVID

So right, like you've got a personal relationship to both character and author, but the contrast between those two personal perspectives makes us doubt the reliability of perspective in general, which renders the *novel's* perspective *im*personal.

SARAH

Or extra-personal. Like *To The Lighthouse*, where time moves slow for the first hundred-fifty pages and then it's suddenly really fast. And then / it's slow again.

> ### DAVID

Right, slows down again.

> *Again, both bells.*

What time is it?

> ### SARAH

Late.

> ### DAVID

Yeah
So you're a [fan of—], you like *Lighthouse*?

> ### SARAH

I love the ending.

> ### DAVID

Remind me what

> ### SARAH

The painter, Lily.

> ### DAVID

Oh the portrait right.

> ### SARAH

She completes it. Finally. And she doesn't need anyone to see what she's done, or that she lived even. Because she did it. She's done it. She's had her vision.

> ### DAVID

"I have had my vision" right. I love that.

> ### SARAH

It's nice.

> *They kiss. (We see it, or we don't.)*

That was nice too.

                    DAVID
Yeah.
So would you— we should get together again some time or...

                    SARAH
Sure.

                    DAVID
Am I, I don't mean to rush it, but—

                    SARAH
                    (maybe checking her stopwatch)
We're married.
We've been married for eighteen years.

                    DAVID
Huh.

                    SARAH
Yeah.

                    DAVID
Wow. Eighteen? So...

                    SARA
So long, thirties.

                    DAVID
Yeah. Gosh. Did you want kids, or...?

                    SARAH
We did. We do.

                    DAVID
Oh.

                    SARAH
Margaret and Lily.

                    DAVID
Oh God.
They're so little.

SARAH

They're young.

DAVID

So fragile. Like I want to cover them in bubble wrap.

SARAH

When we're old, they'll be covering *us*.

DAVID

Yikes.

SARAH

If we live that long.
If *they* do.
If the world doesn't fall apart.

DAVID doesn't like this.

You don't want someone to take care of you?

DAVID

I don't want anyone to have to.

SARAH

That's how it works.

DAVID

I feel so... / [guilty.]

SARAH

When you're lucky.

DAVID

I always thought having kids would— that I'd be bringing life into the world. But really, because of us, because we chose to have them, our children are going to die. We murdered them.

SARAH

You think your parents murdered you?

DAVID

Am I really 52?

                    SARAH
Yeah.

                    DAVID
I feel like I'm seven.

                    SARAH
Fifty years ago.

                    DAVID
Forty-five.

                    SARAH
Lily is. Seven.

                    DAVID
What's she reading now?

                    SARAH
Charlotte's Web.

                    DAVID
I never read it.

                    SARAH
Really?

                    DAVID
I wonder if she'll ever read my books. Or yours.

                    SARAH
                (re: her book)
The Methodology of Narrative?

                    DAVID
She could. She might.

                    SARAH
Not any time soon. I can't believe you never read *Charlotte's Web.*

                    DAVID
I can't believe we elected a fascist.

SARAH

We didn't.

DAVID

My uncle did.

SARAH

Your uncle's an idiot. I'm getting bifocals.

DAVID

Already?

SARAH

It's normal.

DAVID

None of this is normal.

SARAH

"I have had my vision."

DAVID

My heart stopped. I had an attack.

SARAH

It's fine. You're fine.

DAVID

I'm not. I won't be.

SARAH

Nobody lives forever.

DAVID

Thanks for that. Thanks for the reminder.

SARAH

It's true. And it's true that you're OK now, that you're going to be OK.

DAVID

My body is falling apart.

SARAH

You're still young.

> **DAVID**

The country's falling apart. The world is.

> **SARAH**

Not yet. Not completely.

> *SARAH rings her bell.*

My mother died.

> **DAVID**

I'm so sorry.

> **SARAH**

It happens. It happens to everyone.

> **DAVID**

And my father's not, he doesn't even...
What's he doing with that woman? She's younger than *you* are.

> **SARAH**

I'm not that young.

> **DAVID**

When I was a kid I thought I had so much time, stretching out into infinity. Too much. I couldn't wait to get older. To become the person I was going to be.

But now years go by faster than I can count them. And I have no idea where they've gone, or what they meant.

> **SARAH**

We've spent a lot of them together.

> **DAVID**

Yeah.
That's been good.

> *DAVID stops his stopwatch.*
> *He rings his bell.*

> **SARAH**

To find or make meaning from what we remember and who we think we are, we tell stories. And they're always in relation to other narratives, to other people. In dialogue.

SARAH (CONT'D)

But after seeing the world through someone else's words, we sometimes find we're no longer who we thought we were. And now the story is ours and not ours. A double vision.

And that gives me hope. That what we are doesn't exist in a vacuum. That it's only when shaped by each other that we really become ourselves.

Which means that maybe something will outlast us too. Even after we've exhausted our own little vision of the world. That it will live on in some way, for a while at least, through the people we've loved.

Thank you so much for coming. I'm glad we could share this time together.

I know we're all going to miss David very much.

End of play.

Old Beggar Woman

by

Avery Deutsch

AVERY DEUTSCH

Avery Deutsch is a Brooklyn-based actor and playwright. Full-length plays include *The Winterguard Play* (reading at NYTW Nextdoor, Aug 2019), The *Guests and Lucky!* (Developed with Leo Abel, Russell Norris, and Henry Evans at the Orchard Project and Dixon Place). Short plays include *Old Beggar Women* (Winner! Red Bull Short New Play Festival 2020), *The Donor* (Playing on Air Third Place Winner Stevenson Prize 2020), *The Patriot* (acted and performed at Actors Theatre of Louisville as part of the 2018 Solo Mio festival). Avery is a member of Actors Equity and was an acting apprentice at Actors Theatre of Louisville (18/19 PTC).

OLD BEGGAR WOMAN
appeared in the
2020 Red Bull Theater Short New Play Festival:
Private Lives

CAST OF CHARACTERS

Sibyl. Early 70s. Looking for a friend.

Amanda. Early 80s. Looking for a project.

Setting: Two adjacent balconies. A nursing home. The first warm day.
Running Time: Ten minutes.

A NOTE FROM THE AUTHOR

Amanda and Sibyl reunite after years apart, and begin an unlikely study.

OLD BEGGAR WOMAN

Lights up. A very long silence.

SIBYL

It's strange we've both ended up here

AMANDA

Is it?

SIBYL

Isn't it?

AMANDA

Well I don't know.

SIBYL

You don't find it odd?
Out of all the places. In all the cities.
And our balconies next to each other
I mean that's just
That's
I mean there isn't a word for it... but I'd think the best word would be/

AMANDA

Strange?

SIBYL

Precisely.

AMANDA

Well... ok. Yes. It's a little strange.

SIBYL

How long have you been here?

AMANDA

Oh I'm... I'm not quite sure.

SIBYL

A year?

AMANDA

Longer than that

SIBYL

Two years?

AMANDA

A little longer I'd think

SIBYL

Three then?

AMANDA

Yes perhaps. Perhaps three.

SIBYL

I've been here a month

AMANDA

Good to know

SIBYL

I've been here a month
But it's been too cold to go out on the balcony.
I have poor circulation now.
I have a long list of things that don't work anymore but my circulation... my circulation is probably at the
top of the list

AMANDA

How sad

SIBYL

It is sad
I can never feel my feet. It's strange walking around and not being able to feel your feet
Sometimes I like to reach down and put my hand on the floor
Just to make sure

AMANDA

I do that too sometimes

SIBYL

Feel the floor?

AMANDA

No not with the floor
With other things I think might have… gone missing

SIBYL

What kind of things?

AMANDA

Oh it's personal

SIBYL

What? We're old friends!

AMANDA

Are we?

SIBYL

Well we have history
Which is the stuff of friendship
…do you get many visitors?

AMANDA

No.

SIBYL

Me neither

AMANDA

Hence your search for a friend

SIBYL

Well I suppose. Especially with our balconies so near each other.

AMANDA

So what do friends do?
Shall we share?

SIBYL

Yes yes. Let's share.

Silence.

SIBYL (CONT'D)

I don't much like to share

AMANDA

Me neither

SIBYL

Excellent.

AMANDA

Indeed.

SIBYL

You still look very beautiful.

AMANDA

Oh thank you.

SIBYL

You can't say I look beautiful too?

AMANDA

Ok fine you look beautiful.

SIBYL

No I don't

AMANDA

I don't think I look beautiful either so...

SIBYL

What age did you realize you weren't beautiful anymore?

AMANDA

I'm not sure...

SIBYL

I know exactly.

AMANDA

Really

SIBYL

Yes well because I was monitoring it so closely
I checked in the mirror every day
And 13 years ago... I knew
My beauty.
It was just... over.

Beat.

AMANDA

I don't really miss being beautiful

SIBYL

No?

AMANDA

No I don't really miss it.

SIBYL

I'm jealous.
I miss it. So much.
You know how you read stories of people whose husbands or wives have died?
Maybe in some sudden tragic unfortunate way?
And the spouse— who's still alive
They wake up in the night
—And maybe they've had a nightmare
And they wake up yelling their dead spouse's name?
Or you know about people who lose a limb?
And then they have that syndrome
It's called...
Phantom limb!
Yes they have phantom limb syndrome
That's what I'm like with my beauty.
I wake up in the night and for a moment
I think it's still there
And then I realize
That I can't feel my feet
...
And it all comes back.
......
I guess I have Phantom Beauty Syndrome.
Something like that.

Long silence.

AMANDA
Yes I don't feel that way.

SIBYL
Well I envy you

AMANDA
Well that's nice of you to say

SIBYL
So you like it then?
Being old?

AMANDA
Oh no.
Oh of course I don't like it
I don't like it at all.

SIBYL
So do you miss what?
Being agile? Being fit?

AMANDA
A bit. But... no.
The things I miss aren't... aren't nice things

SIBYL
Well I think missing my beauty isn't particularly evolved

AMANDA
No no it's not
It's shallow
But you know
It's also
It's very human you know
To miss something
People told you
Was a gift of yours
Even though being beautiful is no talent
But even things we get just from luck

AMANDA (CONT'D)

It's normal for us
To long for them

SIBYL

Yes yes.
You're right of course.
So what you miss
Was it luck?
Was that how you got it?

AMANDA

I'm not sure...
I mean I clearly had natural inclinations that I suppose were a kind of luck...
But I also made choices
I made choices
To live a certain way

SIBYL

And you miss living that certain way?

AMANDA

Yes. Yes I really do.

SIBYL

And what way was that?

AMANDA

Well I've had a lot of time to think about it
And I've realized that what I liked most of all
What I prioritized again and again and again
Was being cruel

SIBYL

Cruel?

AMANDA

Yes. That's what I loved most of all.
Not to physically be cruel
Although of course from time to time
That has it's joys
But no

AMANDA (CONT'D)

To be verbally

Cruel

To word by word

Rip a person apart

First in little ways

It's all about narrative really

We all carry around these tidy little narratives

About what makes us disgusting and unlovable

And they're always quite simple really

They're always very easy to pin down

I'm stupid or... I lack work-ethic... I'm needy... I'm unstable

And they're always easy to spot

If you're looking

For instance you

You just laid it out for me

That you miss being beautiful

And really that tells me

That you have no self-worth

That someone long ago convinced you

That your greatest gift

Was that people want to fuck you

And so now that people don't want to fuck you

You think you might as well just die

And so anyway...

I've always been able to see those little narratives very quickly

And one step at a time

Press harder and harder into the things a person already believed about themselves

Slowly... But precisely.

Until they took those insecurities not as little passing qualities

But absolute truths.

And then I'd walk away

Always knowing

Without me

They might have been happy

Long silence.

SIBYL

That's what you miss about being young??

AMANDA

Yes. That's what I miss.

SIBYL

That's... disgusting.

AMANDA

I'm sure it is.

SIBYL

And anyway you can... you can still do that can't you? You can be cruel at any age

AMANDA

Yes yes but we don't believe old people you see
So it's harder to exact pain when you're old
It's harder to get underneath people's skin
We're just....
ridiculous old beggar women to them
They are so inclined
To believe that they feel for you.
When actually they just
Don't really want to
see you... at all.
.....

SIBYL

You could be cruel to other old people

AMANDA

Yes

SIBYL

Other old people won't see you as ridiculous

AMANDA

Correct

SIBYL

And in fact other old people are often even more sensitive than the young

AMANDA

Yes I know

Beat.

SIBYL

My room isn't next to you by accident is it?

AMANDA

No

SIBYL

I didn't end up in this home by accident have I?

AMANDA

Not at all

SIBYL

How did you even/

AMANDA

We traveled in very similar circles Sibyl.

SIBYL

So you brought me here
To torment me on this balcony
As I age
And then die?

AMANDA

Not exactly

SIBYL

Then what?

AMANDA

All those years ago...
I thought you were
I thought you were more equal to the task of confronting me than
I had expected

SIBYL

You did?

AMANDA

Yes yes. And when I left you alone with... what's his name?

SIBYL

I can't remember

AMANDA

Me neither
...
But yes
Well I thought
This woman
She got very very close to
Getting under my skin

SIBYL

I did?

AMANDA

Yes.

SIBYL

Huh.

AMANDA

And so I thought.
"She might have some potential"
I found myself filled with a little regret
That I didn't find you sooner
And help you nurture
What I perceived as gifts

SIBYL

So you brought me here to what?
To train me in... the... art of cruelty?

AMANDA

That's well put.
Yes. I have.

SIBYL

Wouldn't it be better to train someone young?

AMANDA

Someone young will not sit with me everyday

All day

You have nowhere else to go

So we'll make a little practice of it here. In our little secluded corner of the world

And hope that it ripples outwards

SIBYL

Why would it be good? For a practice like this to... ripple outward?

AMANDA

Don't you think?

That far too many people

Believe themselves to be good

When in fact perhaps

If we luxuriated a little more in— as you put it!

The art of cruelty

We might not always see ourselves as so

Permanently blameless

...

And. Besides. It's fun.

Beat.

SIBYL

When do we start?

AMANDA

We already have.

End of play.

Love-Adjacent (or Balcony Plays)

by

Leah Maddrie

LEAH MADDRIE

Plays by Leah Maddrie include *Just About Love*, an adaptation of Shakespeare's *All's Well That Ends Well* (Harlem Shakespeare Festival); *Dark Energy Stuns Universe* (Sloan Foundation Award/Ensemble Studio Theater *First Light* Festival); *Middlemuddle* (*Shadow* Festival, La MaMa E.T.C.); and *Chasing Heaven* (Metropolitan Playhouse and New York International Fringe Festival). Her poetry won a Bronx Council on the Arts BRIO Award. Leah was an actor in U.S. theaters coast-to-coast, including the New York Shakespeare Festival, Repertory Theatre of St. Louis, and the Mark Taper Forum in Los Angeles. As an arts administrator, she has worked in development for several New York City cultural institutions, such as Brooklyn Academy of Music, Alvin Ailey Dance Foundation and Lincoln Center Theater. She has a bachelor's in Arts Management from Eastern Michigan University; a master's in Arts Administration from Teachers College, Columbia University; and an M.F.A. in Acting from the University of California, San Diego.

LOVE-ADJACENT (or BALCONY PLAYS)
appeared in the
2020 Red Bull Theater Short New Play Festival:
Private Lives

CRESSIE. Black female, 60ish, a famous writer, educated, regal, dignified, but also warm, reflective, charismatic; brimming with humanity and the desire to connect in spite of the world's evils.

WHITE YOUNG MAN. Age anywhere from 20s to early 40s, Cressie's current lover, educated member of the creative-class, idealistic and progressive, earnest and optimistic about life.

TROY. Black male, 60ish, very successful businessman who created his wealth with honesty and determination; educated, attractive, ambitious, straight and traditionally masculine, dignified, serious, but capably comic as needed.

WHITE YOUNG WOMAN. Female, 20s-early 40s. Plays a notably younger, energetic, nubile partner for Troy. Also plays a maid who introduces this piece in the time-honored tradition of sassy servants in classical comedies such as Molière's work.

Setting/Place: Adjoining balconies of two luxury hotel suites in a very upscale hotel in a major city in the United States in the late 2010s, after the Obama administration has ended but before the 2020 global pandemic, when strangers could kiss, unmasked.

Time: Early evening, as it is slowly getting darker.

Running Time: Ten minutes.

A NOTE FROM THE AUTHOR

Several years after starting my career in theater by acting with a company dedicated to classical work, I challenged myself to write a verse play. I always loved the poetry of the classics. When actors spoke heightened language, it seemed to transport everyone to a new level. I felt that was one of the purposes of theater: to take participants on stage and in the audience to another plane.

I adapted a Shakespeare play I'd appeared in as an actor. I moved the setting to a 20th century moment in African-American history and kept much of the original language, though I eliminated characters and streamlined the plot. With the Red Bull Theater Short New Play Festival, I dared myself to create original scenarios and fresh dialogue on demand, by deadline, inspired by someone else's theme.

After some unsuccessful submissions to the Festival, in 2020, just before the pandemic hit its stride, my play *Love-Adjacent* was selected. The Festival was presented on an online platform that many people across the world got to know well: Zoom. This allowed friends and family across the country to see what I'd been working on as a writer after leaving a decade of professional acting for jobs in arts administration.

The theme for 2020's festival was Noel Coward's *Private Lives*. I wove that in with the tales of Troilus and Cressida and Romeo and Juliet. I added other ideas I'd long been fascinated with: the long-term emotional and social development of Black teenagers who were innocent victims of white violence and rage during civil rights protests, and the keen awareness of mortality that happens in middle-age.

When I read about brave figures like the Little Rock Nine (nine black students who integrated Little Rock High School in the South in the 1950s, enduring mob violence in the streets from white adults and physical aggression in their school from white students), I always wondered about the effect of those unrelenting stresses on their lives. Black heroes of race-related human rights actions are usually depicted— especially for predominately white audiences— as noble, stoic saints who bear beatings, threats, and incessant demoralization with no impact on their mental health or relationships.

We are fully human, of course. I am Black. I know that we have feelings. We thrive with love: familial, romantic, and collegial. We get sad and are hurt from various forms of rejection like anyone else. We can be strong, as we often have to be, but it comes at a price.

Love-Adjacent explores an encounter between two Black people in late middle-age, once high-school sweethearts, who survived the violence of busing for school integration in cities like Boston in the 1970s. I wrote the play in the late 2010s when many thinking people of progressive political temperament were sad and angry about the direction the country seemed to be going in just before the 2020 U.S. Presidential election, when bigotry and hate were encouraged. Could love win in such a climate?

LOVE-ADJACENT
(or BALCONY PLAYS)

*A WHITE FEMALE ACTOR between 20-40 years of
age comes out dressed in a contemporary hotel
maid's uniform. Maybe it is spectacularly
unflattering. Maybe not. Either way, she isn't happy
and lets us know that through her attitude during the
following speech.*

WHITE MAID

It is an honoréd tradition to
Have a maid, such as me, talk to you
Right at the start to tell you what you need
To know so your attention's guaranteed.
I'll start by sayin' somethin' 'bout the time.
(And I'm so sorry that they made me rhyme.)
Two-score years past mid-nineteen seventies,
Teenage affairs are only memories
To Baby Boomers in the twen'y-teens.
In just a moment you'll see what that means.
Now we are gazing at a grand hotel,
Two balconies,

(gesturing between two spaces)
some shrubs here— Got it? Swell—
Where it is easy to hear things next door,
And that, my friends, is what this play calls for.
So to our tale! It will soon be clear
We're riffing on some classical sets here...

Looks at audience member.

That's sets s-e-t-s not "sex" ok?
Don't let your dirty mind get in the way.
Troilus and Cressida are <u>one</u> of the
Romantic pairs behind this brief story
Of Troy and Cressie. Modern private lives
With an imagined future where he thrives.
That don't mean nothin' 'less you know the plot
From Shakespeare or Chaucer. It matters not.

Uncomfortable pause.

WHITE MAID (CONT'D)

I'm back as someone different later on.
But until then I think I'd best be gone.

> *She leaves.*

> *A BLACK WOMAN of about 60 comes out on one of the balconies. She is attractive in a mature way— not perfectly formed to fit the male gaze but with an intense, earthy, grounded, warm but intellectual air. A resignation about life's evils but a defiant resolve to find joy in her later years. She stands looking out at the audience, presumably looking out on the balcony. She is pensive. Talks aloud, to herself.*

CRESSIE

"In sooth I know not why I am so sad."

> *We hear a young-sounding MALE VOICE from the room behind her.*

WHITE YOUNG MAN

I guess I needed that nap. Cressie? Dear?

CRESSIE

Out here.

> *We see him. He is very earnest and cute and wearing a robe. He is not so young that she is robbing the cradle, but young enough to be a fervent leftie with hope, even in deeply conservative times, having not fought earlier battles and been thoroughly demoralized and discouraged by retrenchments.*

WHITE YOUNG MAN

O there you are.

CRESSIE

Yes dear. I'm here.
Just being still.

WHITE YOUNG MAN

And even still sublime.
How 'bout I give you some more quiet time?
I'll freshen up and be out of your way.
Just a few minutes in the shower, ok?

WHITE YOUNG MAN (CONT'D)

The night is young as someone smart once said.
We didn't come here just to lie in bed.
Besides, it'd be impossible to sleep
Considering the company I keep...

He hugs her. They get lost in love.

CRESSIE

I'd given up on love. I'd said, "No more!"
But there you were that day in that bookstore.
I thought that love was just as rare a find
As literary places for the mind.
I figured I'd just sign books in that place
Until I saw your eager, ardent face.

WHITE YOUNG MAN

Who knew I'd end up with so much more than
Your autograph signed with that fancy pen.

CRESSIE

It was the best book signing I've had yet,
And what I took away I don't regret.

WHITE YOUNG MAN

Now here we are. You finally said yes!

CRESSIE

But yes to what? A marriage vow I guess
Without a marriage. Is that what we said?

WHITE YOUNG MAN

We said we don't need to be leg'lly wed.

CRESSIE

Oh right. We're celebrating our two-hood.
Our mutual dependence.

WHITE YOUNG MAN
Is that good?

CRESSIE
Of course it is. What I'd been hoping for.
As long as we care for each other. Sure.
I'm old enough to cherish sincere love.
I want to be together. Be part of...

WHITE YOUNG MAN
A team. A couple. Sacred in its bond.

CRESSIE
Mm-hmnn. Uh-huh. But listen don't abscond
With my heart once you see some flashy bae
Who's half my age...

WHITE YOUNG MAN
  Of course not! I'm your sla... [note: as in "slave"]
I didn't mean that!

CRESSIE
  Haha you are... sweet.
I'm not offended. Long as you don't cheat.

WHITE YOUNG MAN
Well, good because we have so many years
ahead of us.

CRESSIE
(more aware of mortality than he is; ambiguous)
Mm-hmnn. So many years.

> *They kiss for a few beats.*

> *He leaves. She looks out again.*

> *Next-door balcony. A BLACK MAN. A WHITE YOUNGER WOMAN, same actress who played the maid, hugging him playfully, making those "people-in-love PDA" (pretty damned annoying) kissy-face sounds. Note, she is a different character here—maybe differentiated by a wig or costume change or her own physicality and voice adjustments.*

> *The BLACK MAN is exhausted from too much of a good thing at an age when he can barely handle it.*

TROY

I hate to say I think I need a break!

> *CRESSIE starts when she hears the man's voice.*
> *Even more when she hears his name.*

WHITE YOUNG WOMAN

Right, Troy my love! I'll be good for your sake.

> *CRESSIE listens to their exchange. Maybe some*
> *comic business of her going to the hedge to hear*
> *and peek.*

WHITE YOUNG WOMAN

You didn't come here for a passion-fest.
You took time from your businesses to rest.
I'll go downstairs and buy some souvenirs.
If that cute shop's still open...

CRESSIE
(aside)
> I'm all ears!

WHITE YOUNG WOMAN

It might be closed already. Better go.
Give you a break. But I'll be back.

TROY
(overlapping a bit, touching an aching back)

Back... oh!

WHITE YOUNG WOMAN

Parting is such sweet sorrow.

TROY
> Yeah, I know.

> *She leaves.*

> *CRESSIE calls out in a familiar, insistent noise that*
> *had meaning in their courting days. TROY looks over,*
> *startled, recognizing the sound. Goes to the hedge,*
> *parts it. Sees her.*

>> TROY (CONT'D)

O!

>> CRESSIE

> O.

>> TROY

Ah. Cressie. Here!

>> CRESSIE

>> Yes. Do we dare

To speak or is our break beyond repair?

>> TROY

I hope that we both rue those bitter scenes
Around that ugly break-up in our teens,
When you betrayed me to be with that guy...

>> CRESSIE

Believe me, now I often wonder why.

>> TROY

Well. Here we are. Um. Well. May I come over?

>> CRESSIE
>> *(looking toward main room)*

It's not a good time.

>> TROY

>> Oh. I see. A lover.

>>> *"Lover" said with a strange unidentifiable*
>>> *Continental accent that makes it rhyme— if you can*
>>> *pull that off and make it funny!*

Well let me make a wider hole to see...

>>> *Takes chair or something to widen the space so he*
>>> *can see her better. Still they have to struggle to see*
>>> *each other and sometimes are virtually doing*
>>> *monologues.*

Wow. Look at you. You look terrific.

CRESSIE

Me?

TROY

Too many years I brooded. I know now
We were too young to make that solemn vow
That we would stay attached no matter what.
When you were bused to that white high school...

CRESSIE

That!

What was I s'pposed to do? It wasn't fun
Facing attacks each day... I wouldn't run.
I hated those white faces 'til one boy
Was kind to me and brought a bit of joy.
I thought by some odd logic we could win
When people saw our hearts beneath our skin.
Too many folks were evil. Few were nice.

TROY

So dating one? How could you not think twice?
When you were forced to go to there by decree,
You thought you'd fit in more by dumping me?
They were so violent when you went there.
Threw bottles at you. Tried to burn your hair...

CRESSIE

We've been through this before. You know the score.
But let's review the history once more.
How that boy unlike most of them seemed cool
And asked me for a date away from school.
How being hated we were bound by fate
And stubbornly determined we would mate
For life and after high school wed. Of course
It took us less than two years to divorce.
But now who's chasing some pale princess prize?

TROY

Well, when you see that spark in someone's eyes...

CRESSIE

Yes. In a jarring world of black and white
It's priceless to find comfort in the night,
That gentleness that helps us to be strong.
And mine is in the show'r, but not for long.

TROY
(amused; shocked; curious)

O tell me about... them! Can you come 'round?

> *They both realize at the same time the risk. We should hear next few lines in very quick succession.*

CRESSIE

Well <u>he</u> might hear our front door make a sound...

TROY

...and I don't know how long my girl will be
Out of the room to give some space to me...
Well, if she does come back I'll just explain...

CRESSIE

That I'm your high school girlfriend? What's to gain?
She IS your wife?

TROY

Not yet.

CRESSIE
(suddenly reconsidering; liking the idea)

I'll crawl through here...

> *Some business— perhaps amusing— negotiating the hedge until she is on his side.*

So briefly, here's the story, Troy my dear.
He's young. He's woke. He's white. And that's OK.
He gives me hope to face another day.
Though I demand respect, I want love too.
He offered it. I took it. Wouldn't you?
He's cute. He protests in the right parades.
Recycles. Calls me Ms. Does not have AIDS.

CRESSIE (CONT'D)

I guess the years are creeping up too fast.
It feels like Time— Who knows if we will last?
It's just... the melancholy was too much.
I needed something soothing, someone's touch.
So I surrendered to his ardent wooing
Though knowing it was Time I was eschewing.
I'm still quite fond of my first love, you know.
But this is now and that was long ago.

TROY

It's not too late. Not yet. Let's take a spin
At fortune's wheel, let's try our luck again.
I know it's sudden but they're young. They'll heal.
Let's make amends and act on what we feel.

CRESSIE

I just want to be happy—

TROY

I do too
—and celebrate surviving.

CRESSIE

Yes. Yes— Ooh!

They kiss passionately.

I promised I'd be faithful. This is wrong.

TROY

I know. But they'll forget us. Won't take long.

CRESSIE

Oh how I hate to think that! Even so...

TROY

This time it's time to leave your Romeo.
Adventure waits. Let's fly this balcony.

They start to leave. She stops. Warily. Wryly.

CRESSIE

Wait... leave your little Juliet your key.

He does, leaving it on a balcony table or taking it out of his pocket and holding it as he exits. They leave.

Not long after this, WHITE YOUNG WOMAN comes to balcony, distressed.

WHITE YOUNG WOMAN (JULIET)

Troy, darling?

WHITE YOUNG MAN comes out to balcony in towel.

WHITE YOUNG MAN (ROMEO)

Cressie, dear?

WHITE YOUNG WOMAN (JULIET)

Oh! Can it be...?
That WAS my man I saw! He left his key...
Can he... Oh no... I think... He's leaving me!

Both find their way to the still propped-open hedge. Each tries simultaneously to remove the chair propped there and both take each other in and are instantly smitten as both of them have hands on the chair (or whatever is propping open the hedge). Like in a famous play about young lovers.

ROMEO

But soft!

JULIET

Ay me!

(taking in the towel, and more)
O my! Who is't I see?
You're from another play with balcony!
What man are you that so bescreened at night
So stumblest on my... wait, is that line right?

ROMEO

O blessed blessed night! I am afeared
Being in night all this is but a dream
Too flattering sweet to be substantial.
Give me your hands if we be friends...

They touch hands and it grows to more.

ROMEO (CONT'D)

If I profane with my unworthiest hand
This holy shrine the gentle fine is this.
My lips two blushing pilgrims ready stand
To smooth that rough touch with a tender kiss.

> *They kiss. Chair gets in the way. Next line is to audience.*

...And so I say good night for now.
Come on out cast! Time to take a bow.

> *End of play.*

Frankie & Will

by

Talene Monahon

TALENE MONAHON

Talene Monahon is a Brooklyn-based actress and playwright. Her play *How to Load a Musket*, an interview-based exploration of historical reenactors, premiered January 2020 at 59E59, produced by Less than Rent, and was ranked #3 on TheaterMania's list of "The 10 Best Broadway, Off-Broadway, and Virtual Theater Productions of 2020." Her play *Frankie & Will* was produced virtually by MCC Theater during the pandemic and was described in the New York Times as "a witty calling-card." Other plays include *proud revengeful ambitious* (Play Per View) and *All in Good Fun* (Peterborough Players). She is a frequent writer for the 24-Hour Plays, where she has written for performers from SNL and Broadway. Her plays have been developed by Red Bull Theater Company, Cape Cod Theater Project, Rattlestick Theater Company, Roundabout Theater Company, and Northern Stage. Her writing has been featured on McSweeney's Internet Tendency and Points in Case. As an actor, Talene has performed in productions at the Roundabout Theater Company, Playwrights Horizons, the Atlantic, MCC, New Georges, Encores! Off-Center, Red Bull, La Jolla Playhouse, the Huntington Theater Company, Gingold Theater Group, Partial Comfort, and Les Freres Corbusier, as well as selected film and television. B.A.: Senior Fellow at Dartmouth College.

FRANKIE & WILL
appeared in the
2020 Red Bull Theater Short New Play Festival:
Private Lives

CAST OF CHARACTERS

Francis. An unpaid apprentice with The King's Men.

William Shakespeare. A playwright.

Setting: October 1606, London.
Running Time: Twenty minutes.

A NOTE FROM THE AUTHOR

I wrote *Frankie and Will* two weeks into the COVID-19 pandemic. It was produced by MCC Theater as part of their LiveLabs Series in May 2020. The original cast featured Michael Urie as Will, Ryan Spahn as Francis, and President McKinley as Friar Lawrence. The play was directed by Jaki Bradley and shot in Michael and Ryan's apartment, streamed live over zoom using two cameras. It was a lot of fun. It was also missing a major character. Theater is not Theater without the presence of a group of living people, sitting in darkness, breathing all over each other. Whatever we create during this time, it will be lacking for its lacking of that. We missed it during *Frankie and Will.* Shakespeare missed it too, during his quarantined days on Silver Street. At least, I imagine that he did. There is an alchemy to a live audience. They are requisite. Someday, when a new world cracks open, I hope they'll come join this cast.

Original Cast:
William Shakespeare .... Michael Urie
Francis .... Ryan Spahn
Friar Lawrence .... President McKinley

"At this moment is it comforting, or not comforting, to think back to the bubonic plague sweeping through London in the early 1590s, and again, catastrophically, in 1603? Then, too, the authorities closed the theaters in order to stem the tide of infection."

—Sarah Ruhl
The New York Times, March 13th, 2020

"But Shapiro suggests that another closure of theaters, in 1606, allowed Shakespeare, an actor and shareholder in The King's Men, to get a lot of dramatic writing done, meeting the demand for new plays in a busy holiday season at court. According to Shapiro, he churned out King Lear, Macbeth, and Antony and Cleopatra that year."

—Daniel Pollack
Pelzner, The Atlantic, March 14th, 2020

FRANKIE & WILL

A private room upstairs on Silver Street.

There's a desk furnished with a handful of fancy-looking quill pens. An imposing chamber pot in the corner. Loose papers everywhere.

FRANCIS sits at the window, reading a small pamphlet, entitled "King Leir." He is DEEPLY engrossed. Maybe quietly mouths some of the lines as he reads.

The sounds of running footsteps and some undecipherable shouting from out the window.

FRANCIS does not look up.

The sound of blood-curdling screaming from out the window.

FRANCIS does not look up.

WILL
(off)
Francisssss. Fran. Cis.
Frankieee Frankieeeee.

Beat.

Beat.

WILL enters. He is 42 and wears an extravagant bathrobe.

WILL
FRANCIS.

FRANCIS looks up.

FRANCIS
Yes, sir?

WILL
Did you not hear me calling?

FRANCIS
No, sir. Sorry, sir.

WILL

I am in agony, Francis.

FRANCIS

I am sorry I did not hear you, sir. I was reading this play here, sir.

WILL

WHAT PLAY.

FRANCIS

It is called "King Leir," sir.

WILL

What??

FRANCIS

Or, the full title being: "The True Chronicle History of King Leir, and his three daughters, Gonorill, Ragan, and Cordella."

WILL

Where did you get that.

FRANCIS

Here, sir. I believe it is *your* property, Sir.

WILL examines the pamphlet.

WILL

Oh. OHHH. Oh Yes. Yes, I must have acquired that in my extravagant purchasing spree, pre-plague. Along with several decadent ruffs and that well-favoured chamber pot, there.

He admires the chamber pot.

Mm.

FRANCIS

It's very good, sir.

WILL
(still on the chamber pot)
Yes truly, Francis! A remarkably shapely chamber pot, that.

FRANCIS

Oh! Sorry sir. A misunderstanding, sir. The chamber pot is indeed handsome. But when I spake "very good" just now, I was, in fact, referring to this play, sir. I believe the *play* is very good.

WILL
(very quickly)

Who authored it?

FRANCIS

This publication is unauthored, but I believe it is widely known to have been written by Thomas Kyd, sir.

> *WILL throws a quill pen across the room.*

WILL

HACK!

FRANCIS

My apologies, sir.

WILL

I do not mean to unfairly criticize Thomas Kyd's character, Francis, so much as to honestly observe that he is worthless at writing and, more generally, a whore.

FRANCIS

Not everyone has your gifts for language, sir.

> *From out the window: some undecipherable screeching.*
>
> *They stare at each other.*

WILL
(grimly)

Tell me, Francis. What is the news from the world?

FRANCIS

Are you sure you'd like to hear, sir...? Last time I reported to you, you wept and then slapped my face.

WILL

I had been violently struggling to write a sonnet that day.

Beat.

WILL (CONT'D)

Tell me.

FRANCIS

Yes, sir. I will check for you, sir.

He peers out the window.

Hm. I see... three red crosses across the street. No. Four. There is a person painting a fourth cross on the door of the Stilton's house. He is painting the cross. Now he is barring the door with a large bolt.

WILL

OH GOD.

FRANCIS

Ah, I see some physicians!!

WILL
(excited)

Are they wearing their beaks?!?!!

FRANCIS

Yes sir, they all have their beaks fastened to their faces. And they are in their pointed hoods and they are carrying their trusty amulets with blood and crushed-up toads inside. They are exceedingly well prepared, sir. I feel a great comfort just looking at them.

He strains to look around the corner.

Ohhhh, there is a death cart. I see a death cart. It's turning on Silver.

WILL
(scrambling across the room away from the window)

No!

FRANCIS

Yes. There it is.

WILL
(cowering)

No! No!

FRANCIS

It is coming down the street.

(profound)

Oh sir. Something wicked this way comes.

WILL

Well, *obviously*, Francis. It is a death cart.

> *Sounds of the death cart. Wheels turning, people chanting and moaning, general mayhem.*

FRANCIS

I see it, sir. It is quite teeming with its contents. Now it is right below us. Oh sir, it is very stinky. It is moving on. It is going away. It is gone.

> *WILL throws himself against the desk, sighs dramatically.*

WILL

Francis.

FRANCIS

(delicately)

How is the writing going, sir?

WILL

GOD IT IS AGONY, FRANCIS.

FRANCIS

Of course, sir.

WILL

First— and do not take offense, Francis— but I never expected to spend this plague outbreak with *you*.

FRANCIS

I take no offense, sir.

WILL

You are a mere apprentice, Francis! You are a child. You exist wholly to help the players with their lines and also to write down the many inspired turns of phrase I speak when I am too much with drink to hold a quill. You do these things, and we do not pay you, but we feed you, in turn.

FRANCIS

In-turn, sir. Yes. You well describe my lot.

WILL

So, here I am, secluded with only you for company. The playhouses are all closed. I cannot masquerade at the pub. I am distanced socially from my dearest friends and treasured courtesans. And, of course, there's the pressure. There's so much PRESSURE. Francis!

FRANCIS

Pressure, sir?

WILL

Yes! Pressure! During a PLAGUE. To write something truly... unprecedented. Everyone says, *"Oh Will, it's the plague again, I can hardly wait to see what tragedies you produce this time."*

FRANCIS

Oh, sir.

WILL

Every time I go into quarantine, I'm expected to be more prolific and timely than the last time. In 1593, I felt this way!

FRANCIS

I barely remember 1593. I was seven years old then.

WILL

Please do not knead your youth all over my face, Francis.

FRANCIS

Sorry, sir.

WILL

"Knead your youth." Quick. Write that down.

FRANCIS

Yes, sir.

> He grabs a quill and a loose leaf of paper and scribbles.

WILL
(continuing)
Luckily, during the outbreak of 1593, I delivered.

WILL (CONT'D)

I turned to poetry. I wrote *Venus and Adonis*.

FRANCIS

Yes sir.

WILL

And *The Rape of Lucrece*. A STUNNING work.

FRANCIS

I know it well, sir.

WILL
(*reflectively*)
And, I think, a title that will age well.

FRANCIS

Well sir, you triumphed in 1593. And you've written so many excellent works in the time since.
(*a bit suggestively*)
Every young lad of my years would murder to play Juliet.

> *A sudden, high-pitched scream from outside the window.*

WILL

Tell me, Francis. What do you think Ben Jonson is doing right now?

FRANCIS

I know not, sir.

WILL

He is WRITING, Francis! Ben Jonson is notoriously prolific during plagues!

FRANCIS

Indeed. It is much talked of, sir.

WILL

Thomas Middleton is probably at it, too. Probably safely stowed away in a cozy cottage outside of Oxford. Scribbling comedies. And tragedies. And histories. And plays which are confusingly neither like comedies nor tragedies but which everyone loves to love because they think it's provocative to break genre!!

FRANCIS

I must confess, I am partial to that problematic third genre myself, sir.

WILL

WHORESON PEASANTS!

> *WILL throws a stool across the room, then recovers.*

I'm sorry. Francis, I am sorry. It is merely my artistic temperament which suffers being cooped up like this. My sanity is slippery.

> *(gesticulating)*

Write that! Write that! "Sanity. Is. Slippery."

FRANCIS

Slippery. Yes, sir.

> *WILL is gazing at himself in a hand-mirror.*

WILL

Oh, Francis, it is painful to hold, as 'twere, the mirror up to the nature... of my hairline. I have grown old.

FRANCIS

You are a strapping forty-two, sir.

WILL

Francis, the average life expectancy in Elizabethan England IS FORTY-TWO. Have. Perspective!!!!

> *(beat)*

Thank you for the "strapping" though. I perform a strenuous Galliard dance in my room daily to stay slim.

FRANCIS

Yes, sir. I hear you thumping in the mornings.

WILL

And my mouth still retains a few teeth.

> *He shows off his teeth.*

FRANCIS

Oh, sir! I see at least five!

WILL

There are *seven*.

WILL (CONT'D)
(continuing)
Yet, despite my tooth-count, I am tormented. We've been secluded here past all memory.

FRANCIS
Yes, sir. It's been three days now....

WILL
OH GOD. It's the little things I long for, Francis. What I wouldn't give to be in the thick of a good sweaty brawl. Or to be served a decent meal of swan or stork. Pray, what are we eating for supper this evening, Francis?

FRANCIS
There remains a good hunk left of the bread I baked, sir. The sourdough.
(with some pride)
I thought perhaps you might relish some more of it.

WILL
Francis, in sooth, I have grown tired of your sourdough-baking. It is not nearly as impressive a feat as you seem to think it.

FRANCIS
Understood, sir. I suppose we could dine on Friar Lawrence this evening, then?

> He crosses into the next room and returns with a small dog.

WILL
Oh! Yes! Friar Lawrence might be quite tasty. Though rather small.

FRANCIS
(examining dog)
I should think we can pry enough meat from these bones to satisfy your appetite, sir.

WILL
Not a substitute for good stork, though.

FRANCIS
Nothing is, sir. Nothing is.

WILL
Take her away, then.

FRANCIS

Yes, sir.

(to Friar)

C'mon. Out, damned spot.

> *He returns FRIAR LAWRENCE to the adjacent room.*

WILL

FRANCIS?!!!!

FRANCIS

(returning)

Yes?

WILL

Do you think the quarantine will lift tomorrow? Or the day after tomorrow?

FRANCIS

(musing)

Tomorrow, and tomorrow, and tomorrow creeps in a petty pace.

WILL

(snapping his fingers at him)

Francis! Please focus. I must craft a plan.

FRANCIS

With all due respect, sir. Have you ever considered quarantining in the country?

WILL

Yes. Yes. I have considered it. I sometimes contemplate returning to my home in Stratford. My wife, Anne Hathaway, lives there. In Stratford. I suppose, if I wanted to act recklessly, I could head there on someone's horse or donkey or what not...

FRANCIS

Indeed, sir.

WILL

I don't know. It is strange, Francis. *People don't seem to like Anne Hathaway.*

FRANCIS

Mm.

WILL

Have you heard this?!!

FRANCIS

Yes, sir. Bit of a thing, sir.

WILL

God, you are stunningly candid, Francis.

FRANCIS

My apologies, sir. I cannot tell a lie.

WILL

What do you think it is, Francis? That accounts for this phenomenon of unlikability with regards to Anne Hathaway?

FRANCIS

If I may, sir. I believe it to her general demeanor. One feels that she is... acting.

WILL

A woman acting? Haha! A good joke, Francis!! HA HA HA HA.

WILL & FRANCIS

HA HA HA HA HA HA HA HA.

WILL
(continuing)
But I understand your meaning. Though I feel for her in this respect, there's a sort of affectation about her.

FRANCIS

Well observed, sir.

WILL

Yes. Well. We can be objective about this, Francis. As men.

They smile at each other.

Anyways, it's no use about Stratford. I am a city man. And, as such, it seems very natural to me that I should spend the entirety of our marriage apart from her. Given the demands of my writing and my robust pansexuality.

FRANCIS

Both demanding. Yes, sir.

WILL

I will make it up to her though, Francis. I will treat her very nicely in my will.
(thinks)
I shall give her my best bed.

FRANCIS

Sir! What generosity!!

WILL

That's a bit much, isn't it? I shall give her my second-best bed.

FRANCIS

Still a great charity, sir.

> WILL *collects some papers off the ground and stares*
> *at them. He wildly combs his fingers through his hair*
> *a few times; mumbles to himself a bit.*

May I inquire, sir? What is it you have been writing these last many days?

WILL

Francis. I shall confide in you. I have a fancy. For a play. I have written very little thus far. And yet, Francis, I keep returning to this fancy of mine.

FRANCIS

Pray tell. What is your fancy, sir?

WILL

Well. I will tell you.

FRANCIS

Sir, I am rapt, sir.

WILL

(clears his throat)
The tale begins with three witches congregating.

FRANCIS

Witches, sir! Onstage?

WILL

Yes, witches, Francis! It is a tale of dark magic. And jealousy and ambition.

FRANCIS

Ambition!

WILL

Yes. The witches are congregating in a foreign land.

FRANCIS

Which foreign land, sir? Scotland??

WILL

No! No, not Scotland. Uch. Have some imagination, Francis. It is an *imaginary* foreign land.

FRANCIS

Oh.

WILL

Sorry. Did I say three witches? I meant two. This play concerns *two* witches. One witch is golden-haired and bright-natured. The other, inexplicably, has skin of a greenish hue. Due to her toad-like complexion, this green witch is tortured and misunderstood. The story follows the two witches as they form an unlikely but passionate (though sexless) camaraderie.

(musing with excitement)

Perhaps they sing songs, or, when excited, screech wildly... in a sort of musical way. Perhaps the young boy playing the green witch will leap suddenly into the air at some point! In a crude attempt to simulate flight!

(then)

Also. I had the thought this morning: *Monkeys with wings.*

(beat)

That's it. That's the thought. Don't know how, but I'd like to work it in there somewhere. Anyhow. You get the sense of it.

FRANCIS is silent.

Well. Out with it. What do you think?

FRANCIS is silent.

You said just now you cannot tell a lie. Francis!

FRANCIS

Sir. I. I wonder if the public— that is, the public who attends the playhouses— if they would really go for such a thing?

Horrible beat.

WILL suddenly collapses to the floor.

FRANCIS

Oh! Oh sir! Sir...? Are you well, sir?

WILL moans.

Was it my commentary on your fancy that affected you thus...?

WILL writhes on the floor.

WILL

I am hot. Francis! I am hot. Feel my bubous!!!

FRANCIS

Sir, you have no bubous. We have been safely quarantined for days!

WILL feels around his neck.

WILL

I perceive a swelling which may be the start of a bubous. Francis. I insist that you feel.

> He crawls over to FRANCIS and presents his neck.
> Francis feels around his lymph-nodes.

FRANCIS

Perfectly regular, sir. No bubous to speak of.

WILL

The groin, now. Francis! The groin!

> *WILL presents his groin. FRANCIS feels it.*

FRANCIS

Your groin is quite flat, sir. Not a bubous in sight.

WILL
(peeks under his breeches)
Surely it is not ALL flat.

FRANCIS

Sir, you are in a merry mood.

WILL

NOT MERRY NO I AM ILL, FRANCIS. Truly. I feel great dolor of my head.

FRANCIS

Yes sir.

WILL

Now, the pit! The pit!

> *He presents his armpits. FRANCIS reaches for them.*

Heeeheee! Heeheee! Hahahah ho ho Francis, you sly hog!

FRANCIS

Difficult to feel for bubous when you are so delicate to the touch, sir.

> *He reaches again. They begin to tickle each other. It escalates.*

WILL

ENOUGH!

> *WILL pushes FRANCIS to the ground.*

FRANCIS

Well. You seem in fighting shape, sir.

> *(beat)*

I am sorry for my comments regarding your fancy for a play which you confided. Perhaps you are correct. Perhaps this notion of yours— of witches and wild screeching and um, monkeys?

WILL
> *(from floor)*

Monkeys *with* wings.

FRANCIS

Of course, sir. Winged-monkeys and what not— perhaps it *is* what the public will seek. Some day. When the playhouses have re-opened.

WILL

No. Francis, no. I fear you are correct. This plague has found me bereft of inspiration. Do you think Ben Jonson is writing this very minute?

FRANCIS

Impossible to tell, sir.

WILL

Alack Francis, I fear that he is. The great works of this time will be written by Jonson and Middleton and that cream-faced loon, Dekker. *Ooh. That's quite good. I like that. Francis!*

Dictates as FRANCIS scribbles.

"Cream. Faced. Loon."

FRANCIS

Quite provocative, that, sir. Your language is more virile than any of your competitors. Indeed, than any of your predecessors.

He waves the King Leir pamphlet.

Thomas Kyd, included, sir.

WILL
(grabbing the pamphlet)

Let me see that.

"Very good," you said?

FRANCIS

I did think so, yes sir. The writing itself being inferior to your own, of course. But I was myself enthralled to the plot.

WILL flips through the pages.

WILL

Hm. Oh. Oh, yes. I know this one! Yes. The old king. His three daughters. Oh yes. It's coming back. Goneril. Ragan. Cordella.

Makes a face.

Cordella?

FRANCIS

Cordella is my particular favorite, sir. If I may, I saw much of myself in her.

WILL

Francis!

FRANCIS

Sir.

WILL

I have a new fancy.

FRANCIS

Yes, sir? For a play, sir?

WILL

This is my fancy. I shall take this play. "King Leir." And I shall write it. Myself.

FRANCIS

You?

WILL

Yes.

FRANCIS

Sir??

WILL

I shall call it: "King Leir"

FRANCIS

Sorry, sir?

WILL

I shall speak louder. I said: "KING LEIR."

FRANCIS

Sir. Pardon my befuddlement. But it *has* been written? You are holding the very manuscript. Indeed, I believe it to have been written rather recently.

WILL

Yes. Of course, Francis. Let me explain. What I shall do is, I shall take the plot of this play. And the characters therein. And then I shall write the same plot with the same characters. Do you follow?

FRANCIS

Does that not strike you as SOMEWHAT STRANGE, sir?

WILL

No. No. Nothing strange about it.

FRANCIS

I must say, it feels rather morally murky to me, sir.

(musing)

Though, I suppose it is perfectly legal.

WILL

Yes exactly. No rules against this sort of thing! You yourself said the plot was "very good." You spake those very words.

FRANCIS

Might I, sir? Just a thought?

WILL

If you must.

FRANCIS

Perhaps, as you go about the writing of this play, you might make some alterations to the script.

WILL stares at him blankly.

To make it more your own, as it were.

WILL

Ah.

FRANCIS

Just spaking out loud, as it were.

WILL

Oh. No, I see. I see. You make a good point, Francis. What if I altered the title?
(thinks)
I think I would quite like to call my play: "King Lear."

FRANCIS

Sir?????

WILL

My apologies. You did not hear the distinction, Francis. You lack aural sophistication because of your peasant upbringing. What I have done is I have altered the internal letters from "E-I" to "E-A." Thus, adding an "A" and changing Leir to *Lear. My play* shall be called "King Lear."

FRANCIS

This is the change you wish to make…?

WILL

Yes.

Beat.

WILL (CONT'D)

I suppose I could change "Cordella" to "Cordelia." I have an ex named Cordella. I'd rather not keep that name.

FRANCIS

And the other sisters...? Ragan and Goneril? Might you alter those as well?

WILL

No. No. Don't see why I would.

FRANCIS
(giving up)

As you wish, sir.

WILL

Francis! I know that a third of the city's population is perishing right now outside these walls, but I must say, I feel like my regular self again. There is a movement within me. I feel... unblocked!

FRANCIS

I shall fetch the chamber pot, sir!

WILL

Unlocked from WRITING, Francis!

FRANCIS

Ah. This is good news indeed, sir.

WILL

Yes, this play may go down in history, yet. I am quite pleased with myself for thinking of it.

FRANCIS

....

WILL

Of course, you deserve some credit, Frankie. Ha! Does anyone call you Frankie, Francis?

FRANCIS

My mother did, sir. When I was but a mewling youth.

WILL

Mm. Frankie. I feel much endeared to you, Frankie. You will be rewarded for this.

FRANCIS

Perhaps I might play Cordella when the playhouses reopen, sir...? Cordelia, I mean.

WILL

You saucy virgin, Francis. Yes. Yes. Perhaps you might.

They smile at each other.

They stand very close together. Maybe WILL touches FRANCIS' hair.

The sound of another death cart out the window

WILL

What do you think Ben Jonson is doing right now, Francis?

FRANCIS

Tearing his hair for lack of wit, sir.

WILL

And Thomas Middleton?

FRANCIS

Cowering in his cottage.

WILL

Ha! And Dekker?

FRANCIS

Cream-faced as a corpse, sir. Indeed, perhaps he *is* a corpse by now.

WILL

Hahhahahaha! YES Frankie!! Oh, I am giddy. I no longer feel imperiled by the plague-writing of other men.

FRANCIS

Nay, nor that of women, sir!

WILL

FRANKIE.

FRANCIS

Yes, sir?

WILL

Don't be absurd.

FRANCIS

Sorry, sir. I misspoke, sir.

WILL

Women? A woman writing?! During a PLAGUE?

He giggles.

I don't believe they have the constitution for it.

FRANCIS

No, sir. I can't imagine one would get very far.

The sounds of shouting from out the window.

More shouting. Revolution-like shouting.

WILL and FRANCIS stare at one another.

WILL

...do you really think one could?

End of play.

Plague Year

by

Matthew Park

MATTHEW PARK

Matthew Park is a Korean-American playwright. He graduated from New York University's Tisch School of the Arts with a double major in Dramatic Writing and History. During his time there, he concentrated in playwriting and studied under Lucas Hnath, Brandan Jacob-Jenkins, and Eduardo Machado. His thesis play *Hurricane Regan* was directed by Sarah Wansley and performed in NYU's Black Box Theatre. He was Scott Rudin's assistant during the Broadway productions of *Three Tall* Women, *To Kill A Mockingbird* and *Hello, Dolly!*

PLAGUE YEAR
appeared in the
2020 Red Bull Theater Short New Play Festival:
Private Lives

CAST OF CHARACTERS

Mabel. The wife.

Thomas. The husband.

Kit. The lover.

Flagellant. The flagellant.

Setting: In Medieval England a young woman named Mabel ends up quarantined with her domineering husband and newborn daughter in their London home as the Black Plague comes rolling in.

Running Time: Ten minutes.

A NOTE FROM THE AUTHOR

The plays selected for this year's festival were inspired by Noël Coward's *Private Lives*, a classic comedy of manners about lovers and their many foibles. Starring a divorced couple who run into each other while honeymooning with new spouses, it sparkles with Coward's trademark wit. But there's another reason this play has enjoyed such a healthy life onstage: for all its surface delights, it's ultimately a story about how people end up trapped by convention.

Plague Year was also a reaction to the pandemic. I started writing as COVID-19 made its way to the States, and finished a draft when New York was shutting down. This was a harrowing time. In a world gone wrong, I wanted to give someone their power back. Thus, Mabel was born: a smart, resourceful girl who is literally trapped in the Dark Ages. Living under the thumb of a domineering husband, she yearns for freedom but knows that she must play the long game to achieve it. When the Black Plague comes rolling in, she spots an opportunity to escape.

Of course, things don't go exactly as planned. There is always a glitch. But Mabel has spent her entire life backed into a wall, and she always finds a window. She is that person. It's how I saw my own immigrant parents eking out an existence in this country, living the American reality so I could live the dream. They MacGyvered; they pivoted; they found a way. We are the stories we tell. This one is theirs.

PLAGUE YEAR

Medieval London (or thereabouts). A room in a small house of brick and timber. MABEL heats up a stew while her husband THOMAS sits at the table smoking a pipe. A wooden cradle sits between them. Outside, a FLAGELLANT shouts while whipping himself.

FLAGELLANT (OFFSTAGE)

Yea, harken to me! Know that this plague has been sent by the Lord our God to smite the sinners and the heretics! Wickedness shall be purged in the pestilence! The devil's handmaidens will be afflicted with the boils of Egypt, and his servants with the festering sores that laid that great kingdom to waste! Repent, for the wolves are at our door!

Repent, for the end is nigh!

THOMAS

Shut your hole!

THOMAS shuts the window.

Goddamn flagellants. You would think the monks would do something about them.

MABEL

I've heard the monastery has been abandoned. A Spaniard sought refuge within its walls and spread his disease to the friars.

THOMAS

Sanctuary to a Spaniard? Those tonsured fools were asking for the charnel house.

MABEL

It fell on the abbey to house the sick and destitute. There have even been rumors that the sisters provided last rites for the dying, although I have not heard their bells in a fortnight.

THOMAS

Which means that they're rotting in their veils. Serves them right, for thinking women could perform the sacraments. The whole world has gone mad.

MABEL places a bowl of stew on the table.

More pottage? What happened to the boiled pigeon?

MABEL

Went rancid, my lord. As meat tends to do in the summertime.

THOMAS

Well, I can't keep eating this stodgy slop. Now that the serving maid has died you will do your duty as wife and provide me with decent meals. That means veal, lamb or pork followed by sweet custard or strawberry tart.

MABEL

As you wish. It has been difficult since the markets have closed, but I will send word.

> *MABEL moves to pour him some ale, but Thomas grabs her by the waist and seats her on his lap.*

THOMAS

Speaking of strawberry tart—

MABEL

Please, my lord—

> *MABEL struggles in his grasp, knocking over the cup. It falls the ground, waking the baby. She starts to cry. Mabel walks over to the crib.*

THOMAS

That baby is a changeling straight out of hell. She has been crying day and night since the isolation. My patience is growing thin.

MABEL
(taking the baby in her arms)
She is just hungry. Please, have your dinner. I will keep her quiet.

> *THOMAS begrudgingly shovels the pottage in his mouth.*

THOMAS

Now that we have been ordered to stay inside, I have certain expectations. A good fire and a jug of ale aren't enough— I want my feet washed after dinner, I want fresh shirts and clean linens, and at all times I will be well served, well fed and well bedded. I fear sometimes you forget that I am the lord of this house, not that caterwauling little demon.

MABEL

Of course. I will see that all your expectations are met.

> *MABEL puts down the baby, who has quieted.*

MABEL (CONT'D)

Let me fetch a pail for your feet.

> *MABEL retrieves a pail and washcloth from the cupboard. She kneels at his feet and removes his shoes. THOMAS waggles his dirty toes in her face.*

THOMAS

Make sure to get under the nails, too.

> *MABEL begins to clean when suddenly, THOMAS retches. He grabs the pail and begins vomiting.*

MABEL

My lord?

> *THOMAS continues to vomit. He chokes and sputters. It sounds painful. Finally, the vomiting subsides.*

Are you alright?

THOMAS

Dear God. I feel as if I just emptied my bowels through my mouth.

> *MABEL feels his forehead.*

MABEL

Hm. No fever. Do you feel chills? Body aches? Shortness of breath?

THOMAS

What are you doing?

MABEL

You forget that I was a novitiate at the convent before your lordship—

THOMAS

Plucked you?

MABEL

Yes, quite. I studied under sisters of the apothecary. And men don't upend their dinners for no reason. We must make sure you are well. Does it pain you to shake your head?

> **THOMAS**
> *(shaking his head)*

No.

> **MABEL**

Take off your tunic and raise your arms, please.

> *THOMAS complies. She starts feeling under his armpits.*

Does this hurt? Do you feel any sensitivity?

> **THOMAS**

I'm not sure.

> *MABEL pats down his back. She gasps.*

> **MABEL**

Oh no.

> **THOMAS**

What? What is it?!

> **MABEL**

It is a sore. A red pox on your back.

> *THOMAS jumps to his feet. He spins around, trying to get a good look at it.*

> **THOMAS**

No. No, it cannot be.

> **MABEL**

I'm afraid it is. It is small, but I can see it starting to grow. Like a scarlet fungus.

> *MABEL takes a twig from the table and pokes him.*

> **THOMAS**

Ow!

> **MABEL**

The skin around it is already so tender. By tomorrow it shall grow into a tumor. This explains the vomiting: they say it is an early symptom.

> *THOMAS starts pacing.*

THOMAS

What infernal fate is this? Why cast down a man of great stature in the prime of his life when the city is littered with the old, the infirm and the Jewish? What crime have I committed in the eyes of God? The brothels? Oh, Marguerite, a pox on both your pippins! Oh, black day!

> *THOMAS begins to cry.*

MABEL

My love, do not despair. There is still time.

THOMAS

What do you mean?

MABEL

We have caught the disease early; now we will beat it back. You must be treated by Doctor Quackbush.

THOMAS

Dr. Quackbush?

MABEL

They say he studied under the great physicians of Constantinople. He can brew powerful potions out of myrrh and treacle, and his leeches are among the most potent in all of England. He has saved many lives.

THOMAS

Do you think he could help me?

MABEL

If anyone can loosen death's iron grip, it is Dr. Quackbush.

> *MABEL puts his shoes back on. She dresses him in a tunic and drapes a cloak around his shoulders. She sets a linen coif on his head and moves him towards the door.*

THOMAS

But how do I—

MABEL

He resides at the Chancery Inn. Ask for Romilda Ward— she will take you to him.

> *THOMAS tries to kiss her, but she dodges him.*

MABEL (CONT'D)

I will pray until your return, dear husband. God save you! Don't breathe in the fumes!

> *She makes the sign of the cross and pushes him out of the door.*

(under her breath)

Gouty-legged ninnycock.

> *She locks the door and walks over to the window. She watches THOMAS leave, then turns her attention back to her baby.*

Shh, my little darling, you'll understand this one day. When something is wrong, tis best to walk away. And sometimes love isn't love but just a thing that you say, either to keep him happy or to send him away.

> *MABEL places her baby in the cradle. She rocks her back and forth with great tenderness.*

Once you slept in my womb, small and unfurled, but now you are here, alive in the world.

And to survive in the world one must wear many masks, especially girls, for we have many tasks.

Living life in disguise you may feel lost in the shuffle, get trussed up in ruffles, end up in a scuffle.

But know that so long as your mother is here, a confidante you'll have to whom you endear.

As sure as the witches will burn and the rooster will cry, you, my darling daughter, will be the apple of my eye.

> *A knock at the door.*

KIT

Hello? It's Master Parr from next door. I have the pears you requested.

> *MABEL walks to the door.*

MABEL

Simple Simon met a pieman going to the fair.

KIT

Says Simple Simon to the pieman, let me taste your ware.

> *MABEL unlocks the door. She embraces KIT and gives him a long, passionate kiss.*

KIT

My darling, my Héloïse. Did the nightshade work?

MABEL

Yes. He thinks he has fallen ill. I sent him to the Chancery Inn— it will be some time before he figures out what's happened.

KIT

Mabel the brilliant and beautiful.

> *They kiss again. KIT walks inside and pulls out a parcel from his tunic. He places it on the table and unwraps it, revealing two beaklike masks.*

MABEL

Plague masks?

KIT

Protection from the miasma. We cannot ruin your lovely face. Have you started packing?

> *MABEL removes a bag from the cupboard.*

MABEL

Just a minute.

> *MABEL throws various items into the bag.*

KIT

Pack lightly. Essentials only. There won't be much room in the hold.

MABEL

The hold?

KIT

Our ship is bound for the Orient on the afternoon tide.

MABEL

The Orient? But I thought we were leaving for the country.

KIT

Plans have changed. Yarmouth is in ashes. The pestilence destroyed the crops and the livestock— soon all of England will be consumed by the fumes of the dead.

> ### MABEL
>
> But the Orient—

> ### KIT
>
> You will love it there. I hear it is a place of wonder, filled with silk and saffron.

> ### MABEL
>
> We never discussed this.

> ### KIT
>
> Didn't I promise you a new life? Think of it: we could discover a new country and reign as king and queen! You, Gloriana Regina and I, the Second Lionheart. We will have mongols as servants and fire drakes as pets. The monks will write stories about us: the young couple that conquered the East.

> ### MABEL
>
> It's all just so unexpected.

> ### KIT
>
> It's our destiny.

KIT takes MABEL's hands.

From the moment I saw you I knew we were meant to be together. You could not imagine my torment in those early days. I could never stop picturing you in my mind— your eyes, your lips, the dip of your neck— wondering what you were doing, thinking of nothing but ways to become closer to you, to make you mine. And now our future is right on the horizon. What say you?

Pause.

> ### MABEL
>
> Yes. A hundred times, yes. I am ready for an adventure.

KIT swings MABEL around and kisses her.

> ### KIT
>
> Well, come on, make haste! We must get to Bankside before nightfall.

MABEL packs the rest of her things, then walks over to the crib and begins swaddling the baby in blankets.

What are you doing?

> ### MABEL
>
> I will keep her wrapped up until we reach the docks.

KIT

We cannot take her.

MABEL

She's my daughter. I cannot leave her.

KIT

She'll be with her father.

MABEL

Have you gone mad? Thomas isn't fit to raise a child, he can barely wipe his own backside. He would probably sell her to the brothels for a draught of wine.

KIT

They won't let us onboard with a newborn. And besides, she would never survive the trip. It's impossible. Once we are married we can start a new family, with strong, healthy boys who will bear arms.

A silence.

MABEL

You are a liar and a coward.

KIT

Don't be a fool, Mabel. You could not honestly expect me to take the babe with us, to the country or otherwise. She is a sickly little thing, not long for this world.

MABEL

You're just the same. Just another creature of convenience. You thought I was so interesting: the sad, sweet maiden with the flaxen hair, first promised to God and then to a beast in exchange for land and titles. But you don't know what crawls underneath my belly like fleas, the fires that are stoked in the night, the blood that curdles at the dawn. No, you want someone simple with stars in her eyes.

KIT

That is not true. Please, my love, my Héloïse. I want you, no one else.

MABEL

You were always trying to look heroic, so I will let you be generous. Leave the mask— it will protect me. The rest I have no need for.

Pause.

KIT

Fine. Good luck, then. You will sorely need it.

> *KIT leaves. The baby starts to cry. MABEL locks the door, and rocks the baby to sleep.*

MABEL
(rocking the cradle)

Says the pieman to Simple Simon, show me first your penny; says Simple Simon to the pieman, indeed I have not any.

> *The baby quiets. MABEL begins to cry silently, her body wracked with sobs. Outside, the faint sound of bells.*

(to the baby)

Did you hear that?

> *MABEL opens the window. The church bells continue to toll, louder and clearer with each ring.*

It's the abbey.

> *MABEL removes the tablecloth and starts fashioning a makeshift sling. She slips the baby into the cloth pouch. Then, Mabel puts on the plague mask.*
>
> *Outside, the FLAGELLANT continues intoning fire and brimstone.*

FLAGELLANT (OFF STAGE)

Repent, repent! Death is here on his black horse! His pestilence is a scourge upon the land! And at his side is the great harlot of hell, she who has fornicated with the kings and beasts of the earth, drunk with the blood of the saints! Repent, repent! Seek forgiveness and the Lord shall hear from heaven, cleanse us from all unrighteousness, and heal this land.

> *FADE TO BLACK.*
>
> *End of play.*

Something In The Ground

by

Theresa Rebeck

THERESA REBECK

Theresa Rebeck is a prolific and widely produced playwright, whose work can be seen and read throughout the United States and abroad. Last season, her fourth Broadway play premiered on Broadway, making Rebeck the most Broadway-produced female playwright of our time. Other Broadway works include *Dead Accounts, Seminar,* and *Mauritius.* Other notable NY and regional plays include: *Seared* (MCC), *Downstairs* (Primary Stages), *The Scene, The Water's Edge, Loose Knit, The Family of Mann,* and *Spike Heels* (Second Stage), *Bad Dates, The Butterfly Collection,* and *Our House* (Playwrights Horizons), *The Understudy* (Roundabout), *View of the Dome* (NYTW), *What We're Up Against (Women's Project), Omnium Gatherum* (Pulitzer Prize finalist*)*. As a director, her work has been seen at The Alley Theatre (Houston), the REP Company (Delaware); Dorset Theatre Festival, the Orchard Project, and the Folger Theatre. Major film and television projects include *Trouble,* starring Anjelica Huston, Bill Pullman, and David Morse (writer and director); *NYPD Blue,* the NBC series *Smash* (creator), and the upcoming female spy thriller *355* (for Jessica Chastain's production company). As a novelist, Rebeck's books include *Three Girls and Their Brother* and *I'm Glad About You.* Rebeck is the recipient of the William Inge New Voices Playwriting Award, the PEN/Laura Pels Foundation Award, a Lilly Award, and more.

SOMETHING IN THE GROUND
appeared in the
2020 Red Bull Theater Short New Play Festival:
Private Lives

CAST OF CHARACTERS

Lou. 27, at her wits end. She loves her Grandmother's farm but she's tired of breaking her neck supporting it. She values the earth but she needs the money.

Annie. 57, hanging on for dear life to a farm of 10 acres. She knows something's gone wrong with the ground but she can't actually face it and so she rambles.

Sylvia. 72, ferocious, hilarious, and a little bit terrifying. You don't tell her what to do. She owns a 27-acre dairy farm.

Monroe. 64, another farm owner. Although in his 60s, he's still a little randy in the best way possible. He and Sylvia are made for each other.

Setting: The first floor— kitchen and dining area— of an old farmhouse.
Running Time: Ten minutes.

A NOTE FROM THE AUTHOR

The places where there is no punctuation where you would expect it are deliberate. Sometimes too much punctuation leads us all astray.

SOMETHING IN THE GROUND

An old farm house. ANNIE, 57, at the kitchen table. She is drinking a cup of coffee and can't be bothered. LOU, 29, can't believe this.

LOU
She won't get out of bed.

ANNIE
No, she won't get out of bed.

LOU
She has to get out bed.

ANNIE
She says she can't.

LOU
Of course she can.

ANNIE
I don't know what to tell you.

LOU
Tell me she knows she has to get out of bed!

ANNIE
She may know it. That doesn't mean she's going to do it.

LOU exits.

(calling after)
She's not gonna... hell, knock yourself out.

SYLVIA
(off)
Oh no. You get out of here.

LOU
(off)
Get out of that bed!

SYLVIA
(off)
You get out of here! Leave me alone!

LOU
(off)
I'm not going to leave you alone you selfish old freak.

SYLVIA
(off)
Don't you call me names.

LOU
(off)
Freak isn't a name it's a definition.

LOU
(video on)
YOU GET OUT OF THAT BED.

SYLVIA
(off)
I'm sick I tell you! I'm depressed! I'm sad! I'm lonely for the past!

LOU
Well I'm lonely for the future, when you're not in it.

SYLVIA
(video on)
You see. You see what she does to me.

LOU
All right you old witch. You're going to eat this now.
And then you're gong to drink this coffee and then you're going to put actual clothes on, a dress or a shirt and pants, maybe some old shoes, I don't care what you wear as long as it indicates to the larger world that you remember what it's like to be human. You don't have to put makeup on, I'm not asking for miracles. You just have to sit there in clothes. And when that person comes, to meet with you, and have a conversation about what they are going to pay you, for what is in the ground? You are going to listen silently. Like a person who knows that silence is salvation. Is that understood? Don't answer that. I know you understand what I just said. Because I know you know what is going to happen to you if you decide to get clever, or frail or FREAKISH instead of just being silent.

> *LOU exits (video off). SYLVIA starts to eat. ANNIE watches her.*

SYVIA

This is good bacon.

ANNIE

You always liked your bacon.

SYLVIA

Yeah they say on the television that pigs are so smart and it's a shame to eat them, but every time I have a piece of bacon I think well, they're wrong about that. Pigs are delicious.

ANNIE

I had a pet pig once.

SYLVIA

You had a pet pig?

ANNIE

When I was a little girl. It didn't end well.

SYLVIA

Your family ate him?

ANNIE

They sent him off to the butcher, I don't know what happened after that. Henry. His name was Henry.

SYLVIA

Here's to you, Henry.

> *She holds up a piece of bacon and eats it.*

ANNIE

We're not supposed to eat any animals anymore, that's what I heard.

SYLVIA

What damn liberal told you that?

ANNIE

It was on the news.

SYLVIA

Fake news.

ANNIE

You know everyone says that but it can't all be fake news.

SYLVIA

It is all fake news.

ANNIE

But then the people who are saying "fake news," they're fake news too. There was a puzzle my brother taught me about that, when I was little. "That's a lie, the liar said!" So is that a truth or a lie? We used to play that game all the time.

SYLVIA

So if the liar says that's a lie, that's the truth.

ANNIE

That's right!

SYLVIA

How is that a game?

ANNIE

It's just, you know it was kind of a puzzle, like that.

SYLVIA

Not much of a puzzle.

ANNIE

My point being if everyone is saying "fake news" then it's all fake because they're fake news too, so so so

SYLVIA

So it's still okay to eat animals.

ANNIE

I don't want to eat animals. I miss Henry. It makes me heartsick to think of someone eating him up.

SYLVIA

You should never name an animal.

SYLVIA goes as if to exit up the stairs...

ANNIE

Where are you going?

SYLVIA

I'm putting clothes on! Lawyers are coming! Et cetera et cetera. They're selling your farm, the liar said.

ANNIE

She just wants you to talk to them!

SYLVIA

She just wants you to talk to them, the liar said.

ANNIE

Well you're coming back down, aren't you?

SYLVIA

Depends on what the liar says.

(SYLVIA video off) Beat. (ANNIE video on)

ANNIE

Upstairs, she just went upstairs.

LOU

Lord god above I told you to keep an eye on her.

ANNIE

She said she was going up there to get dressed, you told her she had to get dressed! You got to relax.

LOU

I don't want to relax. I'll relax when I have my money.

(to Annie)

Is that the right, what they say there, is that right?

She shoves a handful of legal documents at Annie—

ANNIE

I don't know.

LOU

Just look at them and tell me if they're right, the ones they gave me, are they the same ones they gave you?

ANNIE

Well I don't know what to tell you. This, yes, this looks a lot like the ones they gave me but I can't say for sure.

LOU

That stuff about the the the, what's in the ground?

ANNIE

Molecules, and atoms. They don't mean a thing to me. They're willing to pay for it though.

LOU

A lot. They're willing to pay a lot.

ANNIE

Where does it say that?

LOU

Page 17. They pay you per acre. Is this how much they're paying you?

ANNIE

I would have to look.

LOU

Well look now.

ANNIE

Lou, I don't carry the damn thing around with me!

LOU

Why not? It's worth a lot of money. This number here. That's per acre. That's what they're paying per acre.

ANNIE

If you say so.

LOU

They say so! They're the ones—
How long is she going to take?

ANNIE

You want her to sign it, you got to make it feel like it's her idea to sign it. I'm surprised you don't know this.

LOU

I do know this and I don't care. They're coming today for her to sign it.

ANNIE

I thought we had to go to an office to sign it.

LOU

I told them that she won't go to an office so they have to come here. THEY ARE COMING HERE.

(to Annie)

But that's all the right things, right? You had those lawyers come, look it over?

ANNIE

I didn't have a lawyer.

LOU

They said you had a lawyer look at this, said it was okay.

ANNIE

Who told you that?

LOU

Everybody's saying it! You agreed to this without any lawyer even talking to you about it?

She starts to go through it more desperately.

ANNIE

There were lawyers.

LOU

How many.

ANNIE

One.

LOU

You had one lawyer.

ANNIE

He had some assistants.

LOU

Assistants?

ANNIE

They were lawyers too.

LOU

Are you sure?

ANNIE

There was a big meeting. And lots of people. Well, not that many. But some.

LOU

I want to know, what the lawyers told you

ANNIE

They said the same thing they said to you I guess

LOU

They just said it was the same thing as they said at the meeting, which I wasn't at and neither was she!

ANNIE

It's not my fault you weren't at the meeting.

LOU

Oh my god. But you were at the meeting, Annie, and I wasn't able to be there because I was in the city working eight jobs just so I can keep this place from going under and besides which no one TOLD me about the meeting because the farm is in Sylvia's name and you know she's not a hundred percent reliable so I was hoping that you, maybe, had some notes.

ANNIE

You had to be there.

LOU

But you agreed to this!

ANNIE

I don't know what you are asking. Now. You asked me to come over and talk to Sylvia seven times, or ten times, you were the one who wanted to make this agreement with these people. Now you want to know what it all means?

LOU

I'm asking, I'm asking— you agreed to this! They all said you agreed to it!

ANNIE

Well a lot of people are agreeing. People are agreeing.

LOU

What are they agreeing to?

MONROE enters.

MONROE

Look who it is, look who it is! You looking good girl, all grown up. When you get back into town?

LOU

Are you selling your land to the company?

MONROE

You look good!

LOU

Because I just heard about this, and I can't make head or tails out of it

MONROE

Oh yeah everybody's talking about it.

LOU

Did you show it to a lawyer?

MONROE

They sent us a lawyer for sure.

ANNIE

You want a cup of coffee Monroe?

MONROE

Won't say no.

LOU

So they came last week and talked us through it and left these papers and it's a lot of money

MONROE

Oh you can get more

LOU

What?

MONROE

How much they offering?

LOU

Here, it's in here—

She shows him the pages

MONROE

No this isn't the right number.

LOU

What is the right number?

MONROE

It's a bigger number than this one.

LOU

Are you sure?

MONROE

You got to go a couple rounds with them, is all I'm saying. Where's the page with all the numbers and the letters?

ANNIE

The molecules.

MONROE

That's right the molecules and the atoms. They all think oh they don't know shit, we'll just shove a bunch of molecules at 'em.

ANNIE

We don't know shit, Monroe.

MONROE

But you know what a molecule is. That molecule, that shouldn't be there. They got to pay you for that. Sylvia knows this stuff, she'll know what to do.

MONROE

Where is she?

(yelling)

Sylvia! Are YOU UP?

(to Annie)

Go see if she's up.

ANNIE

I'm not going up there.

SYLVIA

I'M UP.

> She comes out onto the steps, comes down. She is fully dressed.

Hey Monroe.

MONROE

Hey Sylvia. You look good, girl.

SYLVIA

So do you honey.

MONROE

I tell you if I were a younger man, I'd be knocking on your door

SYLVIA

You're still a young man, Monroe, but that's not going to last forever, I'm just letting you know.

LOU

Mom, you have to look at this.

ANNIE

I looked at it, I did look at it and everyone at the meeting said it was a good deal.

MONROE
(looking)

No. No no no. You got to go into the office and tell them forget it, and you're getting your own lawyer. They get all worked up and offer a lot more.

ANNIE

When did you do that?

MONROE

Well you know. It's what they tell you to do.

ANNIE

Who told you to do that?

MONROE

Come on. I saw it on a movie once. But that doesn't make it stupid.

SYLVIA

Let me see it.

LOU

Do not show it to her.

SYLVIA

You already talked enough today.

LOU

You don't know anything.

SYLVIA

No that would be you. You run a farm you have to know a few things.

LOU

Dad ran the farm.

SYLVIA

He's been dead twenty-three years. Did nobody mention that to you?

> MONROE hands her the papers. She starts to look through them.

MONROE

You can get more money than they're offering.

LOU

You saw that in a movie

MONROE

You just said you want the money.

LOU

That is a good number on that piece of paper. They're paying by the acre and we got two thousand acres—

ANNIE

Well Jackie says we should do it.

A beat.

LOU

You showed them to Jackie.

ANNIE

Of course I did.

LOU

Well, that's just— great.

ANNIE

Are you still mad about that?

LOU

I'm not mad about anything. I just don't like her.

ANNIE

You kids used to be best friends.

LOU

Before she revealed her inner true nature.

ANNIE

There's no question she made a lot of mistakes.

LOU

You're a very forgiving person.

ANNI

Not much else to do out here.

MONROE

Tell that to Jackie. She figured out plenty of stuff to do.

ANNIE

Don't start don't don't don't

LOU

She slept with my father!

ANNIE

That's ancient history.

LOU

Oh my GOD.

ANNIE

Don't you oh my god me, I am sick of having this conversation. Everyone makes such a big deal about sex and let me tell you something I'm tired of it. I mean it. Everyone on this whole planet is just done with it and I'm not making that up. It's ridiculous. Who cares who is having sex with who? Who cares where people are putting their penises because that is honestly we all know that that is really what some know-nothing out there cares about, they don't none of them care about what we are all doing with our vaginas or our whatever, our fingers or our toes.

I don't even want to think about it, you want to know the truth. I know what love is. I have felt love for a cat or a dog or a pig, most definitely a pig, that doesn't mean I want to have sexual relations with them. Maybe it isn't love I feel, but whatever it is, it is real and heartful and whatever it is, it has nothing to do with fingers or toes, or or or I know I sound ridiculous and I am not a ridiculous person. I am not happy with my daughter and the way she unmoored this county and the next with her irresponsible and shiftless behavior. But overall all this sex nonsense is nothing important and I refuse to act like it is.

LOU

You're the one who brought her into this.

ANNIE

She's my daughter. What did you think. You asked me if I showed those papers to a lawyer, did you think I would would would

MONROE

Hey Sylvia, you want to go to a movie or something?

SYLVIA

A movie?

MONROE

Yeah, get in my truck and go to the movies. Why not?

SYLVIA

Are you asking me on a date?

LOU

You are not allowed to go to the movies until we get through this! Then you can go to as many movies as you want.

SYLVIA

I'm not signing that.

She drops it on the table.

LOU

Oh. Come on.

SYLVIA

There's nothing on that piece of paper that interests me.

LOU

There is MONEY on that piece of paper! Oh come on. Seriously. COME ON. I NEED A LIFE. I cannot— oh god. I am not. I am exhausted by this.

SYLVIA

You may well be. But that does not make it anything more than fake news.

LOU

That is not fake news!

SYLVIA

It's whatever I say it is.

LOU

It is not, it is not— oh god. It is not—

ANNIE

Look. There's something in the ground here. Is that not a fact? I do not understand why we are arguing about this when there's nothing really to argue about. There are things in the ground. And it's doing things to all of us.

ANNIE (CONT'D)

I don't know why you're still mad at Jackie. She's got the bone cancer. She needs money. We all need money. The land don't give us nothing anymore. We need oh god I don't even know what we need. You look at the television set there's not anything I ever wanted on there, but I don't want what's here either. I know Jackie did stupid things but she's in pain. I want... I want more than fake news that's for sure. I want something now that nobody can give me. Maybe money will do the trick. I don't know. I just don't know.

AL
(at the door)
Mrs. Willoughby? I'm looking for Mrs. Sylvia Willoughby.

End of play.

Evermore Unrest

by

Mallory Jane Weiss

MALLORY JANE WEISS

Mallory Jane Weiss is a NYC-based playwright whose work primarily spirals around female stories, especially as they relate to sexuality, friendship, education, and privilege. Select plays include *Pony Up* (Princess Grace Finalist, 2019; The New School, 2019), *Losing You, Which Is Enough* (workshop readings at The Lark and Cherry Lane Theatre), *A&Z's Escapades in Moonstruck City* (Cutting Ball Theatre Variety Pack Finalist, 2019; The New School, 2018), *Dave and Julia Are Stuck in a Tree* (Playing on Air's James Stevenson Prize 2020), and *Howl From Up High* (Gingold Theatrical Group). Mallory is an alumna of Gingold Theatrical Group's Speakers Corner writers' group and Fresh Ground Pepper's BRB Retreat. She is currently developing a play as a finalist for the 2020 Clubbed Thumb Biennial Commission (*Big Black Sunhats*). Additionally, Mallory works as a teacher/teaching artist, a copywriter, and a cycling instructor. BA: Harvard University, MFA: The New School. www.malloryjaneweiss.com

EVERMORE UNREST
appeared in the
2020 Red Bull Theater Short New Play Festival:
Private Lives

CAST OF CHARACTERS

PENNY. A woman who hates walking through museums; she wants it all, all at once.

WILLIAM. A man with a lot of knowledge about tide pools and other shallow ecosystems; he knew what he wanted but didn't know how to ask for it

Setting: *a series of notes and letters*
> *the green hills*
> *not-too-distant future*

Running Time: Ten minutes.

A NOTE FROM THE AUTHOR

the italics noting what kind of medium the letter is being written on should be read aloud

Sonnet 147: My Love Is As A Fever, Longing Still
by William Shakespeare

My love is as a fever, longing still
For that which longer nurseth the disease,
Feeding on that which doth preserve the ill,
Th' uncertain sickly appetite to please.
My reason, the physician to my love,
Angry that his prescriptions are not kept,
Hath left me, and I desperate now approve
Desire is death, which physic did except.
Past cure I am, now reason is past care,
And frantic-mad with evermore unrest;
My thoughts and my discourse as madmen's are,
At random from the truth vainly expressed:
    For I have sworn thee fair, and thought thee bright,
    Who art as black as hell, as dark as night.

EVERMORE UNREST

The present.

PENNY
Ivory cardstock. Serif font.

The honor of your presence is requested at the marriage of
Penelope Rose Smith
and
Anna Rose O'Malley

an arrow drawn from Anna's middle name, like a stem with a single thorn.
yes, we have the same middle name
I don't want to hear about it.

Ps. I'm sorry we couldn't make your housewarming. It's been too long. Please
come.
Pps. Apologies for, "plus one." I didn't know if Kat spells her name with a "C"
or a "K." Here, I've chosen K, but it looks wrong. Cat? Kat? Cat? Kat? xo

It continues, on the back. Hidden, unless you know me, which he does.

Ppps. I'm going back to the green hills.
open parenthesis. honeymoon. close parenthesis.
I'll check on the bench at our spot. As long as it's safe, of course. As long as
there's time.

WILLIAM
Off-white and textured. three by four inches.

Kindly reply,
regretfully decline.

underline regretfully.

Ps. it's a "C".
Pps. Have fun.

PENNY

A postcard. Green hills and craggy cliffs. The only one that didn't say "Wish you were here." right there, obviously, on the front.

Dearest Will,

Remember our old habit? Of hiding behind ink?
Made it here but haven't seen the hills, which sounds like a honeymoon except for nothing feels like a choice, considering...
Please write back. This room grows stale.
Tussle the air, would you?
xo, Penny.

Ps. "Have fun"? Fuck you.

WILLIAM

Gridded notebook paper. Dated at the top in ballpoint pen. Each number in its own square.
Three days later.

Dear Penny...

I'd nearly kicked the habit.

Cordially,
Will

Ps. Don't have any fun.
Pps. But do be safe.

PENNY

Hotel stationary. Hotel pen. A coffee stain in the corner from hotel coffee.

Dear Will,

Middle of the night. Anna is asleep. I don't want to wake her; but I want her to awake, knowing that something is not right. Knowing that we are under siege. Knowing that the air conspires, that the breeze has surely shifted in the most dangerous direction.
We still haven't seen the hills. All of the hotel employees say it's not safe to leave.

PENNY (CONT'D)

We know they're right; but these hotel windows don't open, and I haven't slept in three nights.

We decided, you and I, to be happy.

Right now, I wish I'd decided to feel safe.

I know I'm not being fair,

you weren't safe at all. you were/are just a man.

I'm sure there's a difference,

but the world is ending, so.

> *The lights shift. Earlier in their relationship.*

WILLIAM

the back of an envelope, taped to the mirror in the bathroom.

Penny, my love,

welcome to your new bathroom.

All the shelves behind this mirror are yours

so you may hide away those magical potions and oils and eyes of newts that make you the unmatchable beauty that you are.

happy moving day,

will.

ps. I've chased out all the shadows and made bargains with all the ghosts. I won't tell you what I owe them. But my debt is well worth coming home to you.

PENNY

Light blue stationary with the phrase "to do" at the top.

a colon. The name Will. A winking face.

handsome,

I've made you pudding. It's in the fridge.

Don't eat it all at once. It's chocolate. It was hard to get.

Save me a bite. Anna promises we'll be done by nine.

xo,

penny

WILLIAM

a yellow post-it on an almost-empty bowl.

oops.

PENNY

a page torn from a yellow legal pad.

turn on the news, you'll see why I'm gone.
forgive me?

WILLIAM

the back of a receipt

I'll be home early.
don't be dressed.

PENNY

the margin of a catalog

miss you

WILLIAM

the corner of page 12 of "Pride and Prejudice"

propriety is overrated.

PENNY

the mirror, in fog

had to meet Anna

WILLIAM

a spiral notebook with perforated edges

Dearest Penny,

A list of things I'd like to do to you:

WILLIAM reads it in a whisper in PENNY's ear.

PENNY

at the bottom of a list that made me blush

have you read about the weather today?
raincheck. pun unintended.
I'm sorry. I'm sorry.

WILLIAM

an index card creased in the corner.

sleep well.
I took the umbrella.
I suspect it'll carry me to work.

PENNY

pen on the palm of my hand.

kiss me.

WILLIAM

crayon on construction paper.

you okay?

PENNY

eight and a half by eleven.

not everything is about us.

WILLIAM

on the back.

I'll keep you safe.

PENNY

underneath.

working late.

WILLIAM

attached.

a question mark.

PENNY

below.

passing ships. until tomorrow.

          WILLIAM

next to.

a sketch of a ship approaching a tidal wave

          PENNY

in my diary.

dearest anna,

          WILLIAM

a bookmark, slid into the page she left open for me to see

I already knew.

          Lights shift. Their first encounter. Earlier.

          The green hills. A bench overlooking them. They both sit for a while. Space between them. WILLIAM sketches. PENNY peels an orange.

          WILLIAM

smells good

          PENNY smiles.

          PENNY

do you want a—?

          WILLIAM

I'm okay.

          He thinks about it for a second.

actually, yeah
I do.

          WILLIAM takes a segment of the orange and pops it in his mouth. PENNY picks at hers until it's completely free from white strings.

that's something I'm working on
asking for what I want.

PENNY

give me your number
I'd like to teach you.

> *WILLIAM writes his phone number down and hands it to PENNY. He begins writing something on the bench.*

WILLIAM

Did you know...

PENNY

Are you writing on the bench?

WILLIAM

Maybe.

PENNY

That's vandalism.

WILLIAM

For posterity.

PENNY

I see.
Did I know... what?

WILLIAM

when they first discovered the green hills,
they thought they'd just discovered a ravine?
steep, overgrown walls on either side.
trapped in a groove on the Earth's fingerprint

> *Back to the present. PENNY picks up the hotel phone. Dials. As it rings, she peels an orange. WILLIAM picks up.*

WILLIAM

hello?

PENNY

did I wake you?

WILLIAM

I was up

PENNY

of course you were
evermore unrest

WILLIAM

it's late for you

PENNY

I was writing you a letter

WILLIAM

this is faster

PENNY

time is of the essence

WILLIAM

don't start

PENNY

I can't help it

> PENNY eats an orange segment.

WILLIAM

eating an orange?

PENNY

they're safe
they come with armor

WILLIAM

it's going to take you an hour to finish it,
the way you pick it clean

PENNY

I thought I had plenty of time

WILLIAM

you do

> PENNY

what if we don't?

> WILLIAM

what would you change?

> *Beat.*

> PENNY

I'd change the way this feels

> WILLIAM

but not the way things are?

> PENNY

is that allowed?

> *WILLIAM shrugs. PENNY can hear it through the
> phone.*

what was the end of that story about the green hills
they thought it was a ravine
how did they discover it was more?

> WILLIAM

they kept walking

> PENNY

that was it?
that's too easy.

> WILLIAM

says the woman who drags her feet through every museum she's ever been in

> PENNY

that's different
that's the past

> WILLIAM

of course.
my mistake.

> *Beat.*

PENNY

you know me too well.

Beat.

WILLIAM

Do you think you'll get to go back?
To see what we wrote?

As the sun comes up through the hotel window.

PENNY

I'm not sure.
There's still a lot I haven't seen, since we've been here.
Haven't seen anything really. The room is starting to smell like us.

WILLIAM

sounds like a honeymoon.

Beat.

send me a postcard

PENNY

I will.
Tomorrow.
When I get tired of walking.

End of play.

ABOUT STAGE RIGHTS

Based in Los Angeles and founded in 2000, Stage Rights is one of the foremost independent theatrical publishers in the United States, providing stage performance rights for a wide range of plays and musicals to theater companies, schools, and other producing organizations across the country and internationally. As a licensing agent, Stage Rights is committed to providing each producer the tools they need for financial and artistic success. Stage Rights is dedicated to the future of live theatre, offering special programs that champion new theatrical works.

To view all of our current plays and musicals, visit:

www.stagerights.com

Made in the USA
Columbia, SC
27 September 2021